IT'S ALL GOOD!

Successfully Living Your *Whole* Life Long

To Gregg!
It's all good!

IT'S ALL GOOD!

Successfully Living Your *Whole* Life Long

by

Bishop Jim Earl Swilley

It's All Good!
Successfully Living Your Whole Life Long
ISBN 0-9716838-4-0
Copyright © 2004 by Jim Earl Swilley

Printer: United Book Press, Inc., Baltimore, MD
Cover designer: Chris Haler • Current Events Productions • Covington, GA
Cover photos: Chris Haler, Teri Haler • Current Events Productions
Technical/Production Editors: René Babcock, Jane Conyers, Robyn Darby

Published by Church In The Now Publishing
1873 Iris Drive, SE
Conyers, GA 30013

Take note that the name satan and related names are not capitalized, as we do not recognize him as either supreme nor revered, to the point of violating grammatical rules.

Contents

All: the total entity or extent of
the entire or total number
every
each and every thing
totality
wholly
entirely
complete
each
exclusively

Good: having positive or desirable qualities
not bad or poor
serving the end desired
suitable
not spoiled or ruined
in excellent condition
superior to the average
of high quality
beneficial

Introduction

This Is Your Life!

And we know that all things work together for good to those who love God, to those who are the called according to His purpose.
Romans 8:28 – NKJV

> Don't **think** you are, **know** you are!
> – Morpheus to Neo in *The Matrix*

Do you know who you are? I mean, do you know who you *really* are? Has your life experience helped you develop an understanding of how the various components of your unique existence intricately work together to create your own personal identity? In other words, have you arrived at the point on your journey where you can begin to see the formation of a big picture – an unfolding of a master plan – without being too bogged down with yesterday's unfinished business, today's uncertainty, and/or anxiety about tomorrow? Can you embrace your past, present and future with equal appreciation so that you are able to come to terms with your *whole* life? In reviewing your biography, can you honestly say that you wouldn't change a thing about the story so far? Has God's goodness become so personally evident to you that you wouldn't trade places with anyone else in the world, even if you could?

Jesus Christ could certainly answer each of these questions in the affirmative. He provided us the perfect example of a man who truly knew Himself, realized the potential of His gifts, and understood the complexities of His own purpose-filled life. Possessing absolute self-awareness throughout the entirety of His earth-walk, He successfully executed His assignment on this planet with an unshakable confidence that ultimately produced (and continues to produce) positive results. It was the kind of confidence that can only come from a person's ability to grasp a real comprehension of where he/she has **been**, where he/she **is,** and where he/she is **going**. *("Jesus answered and said to them, 'Even if I bear witness of Myself, My witness is true, for I know where I came from and where I am going; but you do not know where I come from and where I am going.'" – John 8:14).* Jesus was perfectly at peace with His own life.

You have not picked up this book by accident. There are things contained in these pages that you need to know, or that you need to be reminded of, that will enable you to become better equipped to live out your days with the full awareness that yours is a good life, because it demonstrates that God really is a good God! The truths recorded here can help you learn to say with conviction, once and for all, without denial or disconnection from reality, that the verdict concerning the sum total of your life is this: **It's *all* good!** Regardless of what has or hasn't happened to you, regardless of your own mistakes and missteps, the revelation of God's ultimate purpose for you is designed to bring you to this conclusion: **It's *all* good**, every bit of it! Without regrets or second-guessing your life-choices, or even having all the answers, you really *can* know who you are and you, too, can be perfectly at peace with *your* life!

Some years ago I delivered a series of sermons at Church In The Now ("CITN") entitled, "Living Your Whole Life Long," in which I explored how the past, present and future of an individual all work together to bring about a revelation of their Kingdom life in the now. The teaching was birthed during a time of particularly prophetic significance for us. But in many ways, I feel that the teaching was then somewhat ahead of its time and that now is the right season for me to revisit those themes, to mine out even deeper relevant truths from the treasury of my own eternal life, and to translate them into this format. Not only is writing truly one of the greatest joys of my life, I do believe that there is a certain authority resident in the written page that is superior to that of a sound recording. The point is that the said teaching series did serve as the inspiration for this book, but that this book is much more than that teaching.

The Plan for Your Life / The Plan for This Book

There really *is* a plan for your life, and it's not as hard to find as you might think. God cares about the details of your life because He designed it for purpose – *His* purpose – and that's why He wants to cause all things to work together for your good. He miraculously works the things that concern you together for your good because He loves you, but also because it serves His *purpose* to do so. In these twenty-one chapters, we will examine how He has been working through your past and present together, and how He is even working the future things that haven't technically happened yet, to prove His goodness *to* you and *through* you. The wisdom contained here is manifested as principles revealed line upon line, precept upon precept, and all of them point to His goodness. Proverbs 9:1 says that: *"Wisdom has built her house, she has hewn out her seven pillars."* The seven "pillars" on which *this* house is built are these:

Pillar 1   Your life is *whole.*

 As the combination of your spirit, your soul, and your body create your entire existence, so the combined realities of your past, your present, and your future serve to create your *whole* life. God is in the now, and you are in the now. God reveals Himself by saying, "I am that I am" and as you see His nature becoming more evident in yourself, you will more easily accept that you "are that you are." You are who you *always have been*, you are who you *currently are,* and you are who you *will be* in the future – and you are all of that *now*! The purpose of this book is to help you integrate these three dimensions so that you can live your *whole* life without any fragmentation. The Word of God is *now*, and as your life becomes increasingly more conformed to it, you will cease to view your life as divided into different dispensations and will become more readily able to submit *all* of it to the Lordship of Jesus.

Pillar 2   Your life is *eternal.*

Jesus talked to Nicodemus about a "new birth," and Paul talked about a "new man" who, in Christ, becomes a "new creature" and experiences *all* things becoming new. When you combine these concepts with John's revelation about a believer passing from death unto life, it's easy to accept the basis for a fundamentalist paradigm concerning the beginning of eternal life. The conventional wisdom is that eternal life begins when someone is "saved" or "born again." But eternal things have no beginning or ending – that's why they are *eternal.* So, as important as it is for you as an individual to awaken to righteousness via the cross of Jesus Christ, the gospel truth is that you were chosen in Him **before** the foundation of the world! John's admonition to let that abide in you which you heard **from the beginning** (1 John 2:24) supports the idea that your life was eternal, even before you knew that it was.

Pillar 3   Your life is *unique.*

There is nobody like you. No one has ever had your exact experiences played out in your particular circumstances, so no one can completely understand the way you think, because they can't empathize with how your life-experience has shaped your world-view. You are who you are, mainly because of what has happened to you, and no one, not even those closest to you, can completely know you. That is, no one except Jesus, your great High Priest. He understands you and your life better than you do and He has given you the Keys of the Kingdom to help you unlock your own personal mysteries. The better you understand your life, the more you will be able to enjoy it as it *is,* with all of its realities, and will even be able to effectively improve it. Uniqueness of life makes being envious or judgmental of others irrelevant and exalts the importance of unconditional love.

Pillar 4   Your life is *real.*

You have a personal destiny and it is important that you pursue living it to its full potential. The contribution that *your* life makes is as important in the real world as that of high profile, influential people like Mother Teresa or Dr. Martin Luther King, Jr. Not everyone is called to do things on such a grand scale as people like them, but your destiny is no less important than theirs. The embracing of *your* life with an **"it's all good"** attitude is not a compromise or settling for mediocrity. Today, with such an abundance of teaching on subjects like destiny and purpose, it's easy to forget that each individual can only be expected to become the best version of himself/herself that he/she can become. The world needs *real* people who are fulfilled living *their* real lives – people who realize that even the most "normal" life can be full of excitement and adventure when it is properly discerned.

Pillar 5   Your life is *transcendant.*

When you learn to always expect things to work together for your good, you will find it unnecessary to waste your time in self-pity when things don't seem to be going well for you. The belief that your story will eventually and inevitably have a happy ending makes it virtually impossible to maintain a victim mentality, because your mind can actually be trained to think positively and to respond proactively to all the circumstances of life. The just shall live by faith – the God-kind of faith – the faith that empowers you to live the kind of existence that people who are bound by the limitations of the natural world can't even comprehend. You don't have to settle for less. You don't have to lower the bar. You can realize your dreams and see your faith change the course of events in the world around you. You don't have to live in failure or defeat. You can *excel* in life!

Pillar 6   Your life is *yours.*

God has given you your life to do with, for the most part, as you see fit. If you give your life to *Him,* it will be because you exercised your right to *decide* to do so. Of course, your life *should* belong to God, but the giving up of control to Him is something that is up to you. The ultimate act of sovereignty is that the Sovereign of the universe created sovereign beings after His own kind and gave them dominion in their own realm. Your life is all that you have, so it is imperative that you take ownership of it and refuse to let others run it. The purpose of the existence of all creation is for the glory of God and to give Him pleasure, but the greatest joy in life is discovering that you can serve God because you *want* to. He desires to co-labor *with* you as the senior partner, but He's working all things together for your good so that *you* can dominate and help His will to be done on earth as it is in heaven.

Pillar 7   Your life is *good.*

This is the book's foundational truth and main point. Each chapter begins with a different translation* of Romans 8:28, which states that *all* things work together for the **GOOD** of those who find their purpose in God, and in loving Him. Your past, present and future work together for good! The positive *and* the negative influences in your life work together for good! The triumphs *and* the failures, the victories *and* the defeats, the right moves *and* the mistakes – all of it – work together to prompt you to say when you view your life – **IT'S *ALL* GOOD!** When you fully grasp this, you can let go of your regrets, cease to envy the lives of others, stop complaining about your situation, become truly thankful in all things, live in the now, and become an inspiration to others and a blessing to humanity. It's your time, though you are timeless, to embrace the truth and begin to truly live *your* good life!

*Not every translator chooses to capitalize the pronouns referring to God (He, His, Him), but it is the preference of this author to take license, and to do so in each translation used.

SECTION ONE

PURSUING PEACE WITH YOUR PAST

Pursuing peace with your past is the first step to successfully living your whole life.

·Y·E·S·T·E·R·D·A·Y·

·**Y**· is for **Youth.** *Do not remember the sins of my **youth**, nor my transgressions; according to Your mercy remember me, for your goodness' sake, O Lord. (Psalm 25:7)*

... make peace with your **youth** ...
"Jesus said, '*Let the little children come to Me, and do not forbid them; for of such is the kingdom.*'" *(Matthew 19:14)*

... let the child in you come to Him without fear,
for that's how the Kingdom will be revealed in you ...

·**E**· is for **Experience.** *... Please stay, if I have found favor in your eyes, for I have learned by **experience** that the Lord has blessed me for your sake. (Genesis 30:27)*

... make peace with the lessons that you've learned,
even if you've learned them through the **experience**
of pain and heartache ...

·**S**· is for **Seasons.** *To everything there is a **season**, and a time for every purpose under heaven. (Ecclesiastes 3:1)*

... make peace with all of the bygone **seasons** of your life,
and rejoice that, for every one that has ended,
a new one has begun ...

·**T**· is for **Time.** *Redeeming the **time,** because the days are evil. (Ephesians 5:16)*

... make peace with **time** past,
for God has been there for you all along ...

◦**E**◦ **is for Errors.** *Who can understand his* **errors?** *Cleanse me from secret faults. Keep back your servant also from presumptuous sins . . . (Psalm 19:12, 13)*

. . . make peace with your own **errors**,
for somehow even *they* have worked together for your good . . .

◦**R**◦ **is for Remembering.** *Do not* **remember** *the former things, nor consider the things of old. (Isaiah 43:18)*

. . . make peace with your memories,
but do not feel obligated to **remember** those things that you
know should be forgotten by now . . .

◦**D**◦ **is for Days.** *So teach us to number our* **days,** *that we may gain a heart of wisdom. (Psalm 90:12)*

. . . make peace with **days** gone by,
for each one was one that the Lord made, and you can *still*
rejoice and be glad in them all because of the wisdom that they
helped you to acquire . . .

◦**A**◦ **is for Always.** *For this reason I will not be negligent to remind you* **always** *of these things, though you know and are established in present truth. (2 Peter 1:12)*

. . . make peace with the fact that you will **always** need to be
reminded of the important things that you already know are true,
even though you have heard them many times in the past . . .

◦**Y**◦ **is for Years.** *So I will restore to you the* **years** *. . . (Joel 2:25)*

. . . make peace with all the **years** of your life,
for, one by one, they have each brought you closer to the
realization of your destiny . . .

Reality is a question of perspective; the further you get from the past, the more concrete and plausible it seems – but as you approach the present, it inevitably seems incredible.

– Salman Rushdie

Chapter One

Encountering Spiritual Time Travel

We are assured and know that [God being a partner in their labor] all things work together and are [fitting into a plan] for good to and for those who love God and are called according to [His] design and purpose.
Romans 8:28 – AMP

> It is possible to believe that all the past is but the beginning of a beginning, and that all that is and has been is but the twilight of the dawn. It is possible to believe that all the human mind has ever accomplished is but the dream before the awakening.
> – H. G. Wells

I've never in my life been what you would call a Science Fiction *fan*, per se, but I *have* always been extremely interested in, and fascinated by, the notion and idea of time travel. Books and/or movies on the subject were captivating to me as a child and, even today, I find that I am still drawn to the subject matter, even though my adult mind realizes that the possibility of *actual* time travel is just a fantasy. In recent years there have been many good movies made of the *Back To The Future* genre, where someone travels to the past to remedy a problem in the present, and that particular aspect of the time travel theme intrigues me. I'll discuss this idea further in Chapter Seven, but the point is that people clearly long to connect with eternity and to be empowered by transcending time, and, therefore, stories continue to be written about the subject. The earth is filled with the knowledge of the Lord more than we realize.

In my early years, when I was fortunate enough to have other kids to play with, my number one activity suggestion was always to pretend like we had a time machine that could allow us to visit the distant *past* to fight dinosaurs, or the distant *future* to travel around in spaceships. I loved when Mr. Peabody would take his assistant, Sherman, on trips via his "Wayback" Machine on *The Rocky and Bullwinkle Show*. Those in my age group will remember the poorly (over)acted and ridiculously campy, gothic soap opera *Dark Shadows* that ran in the late 60's. I am rather ashamed to admit that I never missed an episode – not just because it was very badly produced, but because it explored a lot of ghoulish and macabre themes. But the appeal for *me* was all of its time travel plot lines, following the lives of people who co-existed in parallel universes at the same place in different times. That just really worked for me.

When I talk about *spiritual* time travel, I'm not suggesting, of course, that God will enable you to actually travel like some Christian "Marty McFly" into your past and start changing things. What I *am* referring to is developing a certain expertise in navigating through past, present and future knowledge, while staying in the now, for Kingdom purposes. I'm talking about the power to discern eternity – about being able to step outside of time and space limitations *in the Spirit,* and bring your life into wholeness by seeing it from God's vantage point. To me, it is not a contradiction in terms to say that you must *move on* from the past, but that you must also *embrace* the past to understand how to live in the present *and* in the future. For instance, I hear people say quite often that you haven't *forgiven* until you've *forgotten,* and I'm not sure that is a true statement, even for Christians (more about that later).

The Syrophoenician woman of Matthew, chapter 15 and Mark, chapter 7, was a time-traveler. When Jesus refused to cast the demon out of her daughter because she was a gentile (*". . . I was not sent except to the lost sheep of the house of Israel" – Matthew 15:24*), and even, in a round-about way, called her a *dog*, He was not just being racist or simply testing her faith. What He *was* saying to her, in effect, was: *It is not lawful, yet, for me to minister to you in this way. I will preach to Israel for three years, they will reject and crucify me, and then I will be raised from the dead, reconciling all people to God. After that, the Holy Spirit will be poured out on all ethnic groups on the Day of Pentecost, and, later, a man named Saul of Tarsus will be converted and will become the apostle to the gentiles. Then, and only then, will I be able to minister to your daughter, legally. Your premature faith is ahead of schedule!*

But this visionary woman pressed Jesus and, by her tenacious, faith-filled words, was able to reach into her future to make contact with a promise that would eventually be hers anyway. This is what I mean by spiritual time-travel. If you are promised something in the future, but you need it *now*, it is possible to visit the future by faith and bring that thing back to the present. Really, this is what Jesus meant, in a way, when He commanded His disciples to pray, let *"Your will be done on earth as it is in heaven."* If heaven is in your future, but you need the blessings of heaven *now*, you can make a little prayer-trip into the sweet by and by and take care of business. For example, in heaven you will have a perfect, glorified body, but if you need healing in your *present* body, you can make a demand on the promise of your *future* body by believing for healing now! As the song says: *". . . oh, what a foretaste of glory divine!"*

No Place Like Home

I was born in Atlanta, Georgia, and have lived in or near it for my entire life. (It is debatable whether or not Conyers/Covington, the home of Church In The Now and where I now reside, is really *part* of Metropolitan Atlanta, but for the sake of this material, I'll say here that it is). Over the years I have been blessed to be able to travel around the world, and there are many cities and countries that I love to visit as often as possible, but Atlanta is my home and, I feel sure, always will be. It is where I want to live.

Without a doubt, my relationship with "the South" is complicated and conflicted, but I do understand it (even the parts of it that I disdain), and probably identify with it more than I care to admit. The South is what it is, and I can live with it and even appreciate it, even with all of its idiosyncrasies. But, in my mind, Atlanta is *different* from "the South" in that it is so much more progressive than its surroundings.

As I grow older, the city of my birth seems increasingly more to me like an old, cherished friend with whom I share too many treasured memories to count. (If you are not from the area, this part may be lost on you, but) I remember when the scariest ride at Six Flags Over Georgia was the Dahlonega Mine Train, Lenox Square was an open-air mall, and Officer Don's *Popeye Club* aired on WSB every weekday afternoon at 4:30. I still recall, before the days of political correctness, when Stone Mountain Park daily presented a dramatic mock Indian attack on their steam engine locomotive, and Chief Nock-a-Homa performed a victory dance around his tepee every time a Brave hit a home run at Atlanta-Fulton County Stadium. Two of my most favorite Atlanta memories are being at the game when Hank Aaron hit number 715, and Martin Luther King, Sr. giving the keynote address at my high school graduation.

For me, Atlanta represents the past, present and future, simultaneously. For example, I was born downtown at Crawford W. Long Hospital and, for some reason or another, I still find myself having to be at the place of my origin on a fairly regular basis. The first theatre that I can remember seeing a movie at was the "fabulous Fox," and I still frequent the Fox Theatre and love it now more than ever. I still eat at the Varsity and at Mary Mac's Tea Room as much as I ever did. My first sermon was preached at what is now The Abbey Restaurant; the first funeral that I conducted was at Patterson's on Spring Street (where Margaret Mitchell's funeral was); and the first open-air meeting at which I ever spoke was in Piedmont Park. All these places and things are as much a part of my present experience as they are a part of my past experience, and I suppose they are a part of my future experience, as well.

For Atlanta natives only: Before I continue making my point about time travel, here are some more memories that you might share with me . . . riding the Pink Pig every Christmas at the downtown Rich's store . . . enjoying the ice skating rink and *World of Syd and Marty Croft* at the Omni . . . *Now Explosion* - Channel 36's precursor to MTV . . . getting nauseous at the Chevy Show and then totally sick on the Spindle Top . . . watching (and being terrified by) *The Friday Night Shocker with Bestoink Dooley* . . . Flossie Mae taking your curbside food order . . . "Whaddayahave? Whaddayahave?" . . . WJRJ - Channel 17 before it was the Superstation . . . Lion Country Safari . . . Willie B. and the old Grant Park Zoo . . . the *Green Sheet* in <u>The Atlanta Journal</u> . . . riding around 10th Street to gawk at hippies . . . <u>The Great Speckled Bird</u> . . . The Agora Ballroom . . . saving the Fox . . . and "the Centennial Olympics goes to . . . Atlanta!"

My apologies to those reading this book who are not familiar with my hometown – I certainly don't mean to make you feel excluded. But, if you have lived in one place all of your life, or for an extended period of time, you will know exactly what I mean about the past, present and future co-existing there, simultaneously, *wherever* that may be. And yet, for *all* of us, the place that I am describing is really in the spirit realm, or in the "inner man," which is comprised of the soul and the spirit. Your total awareness of eternity lies dormant in your spirit. This is where you truly make contact with the living God. And your *memory* (the passageway to the past) and your *vision* (the freeway to the future) reside together within your soul. This is where you make peace with your life by coming to terms with yourself. The Word of God divides the soul and spirit (Hebrews 4:12), so that you can keep it all in proper perspective.

The Story of Your Life

A good, well-written story has a beginning, a middle part, and an ending, and the story of your life is well written (it *has* been written and is still *being* written) by the Author and Finisher of your faith. Jesus taught in parables and He still does. As He told the stories of the Prodigal Son and the Lost Sheep, etc. to the multitudes, He is also telling the story of *you* to the principalities and powers of the air, as well as to the world around you! He has declared the end from the beginning – for you! He ever lives to make intercession for you, to save you to the uttermost! *"For I know the thoughts that I think toward you, says the Lord, thoughts of peace and not of evil, to give you a future and a hope" (Jeremiah 29:11)*. God wants to give you a *future*, but you'll have to make it through your past and present to get there! He who began a good work in you will continue to perform it until the Day of the Lord. **It's *all* good!**

The story of your life has many chapters, and every one of them is necessary for the revealing of a theme about God in the now. It is written: *". . . there is a time [appointed] for every matter and purpose and for every work" (Ecclesiastes 3:17 AMP)*. The power of memory and vision can enable you to put *the now* into perspective. With the eye of truth you can see into the distant past and solve the mysteries of your life – and with the eye of faith you can see into the distant future and declare the end from the beginning. Travel back in your memory to get in touch with your childhood, knowing that Jesus made childlike-ness a requirement for entrance into the Kingdom. The imagination, innocence, playfulness, and sense of wonder of your youth still remain buried in your subconscious (spirit), and the keys of the Kingdom are available to unlock the prophetic imagery that is produced by the positive parts of your past.

Listen to the messages that your dreams and night-visions convey to you. Instead of being haunted by horrible images from yesterday, recognize that your soul is bringing these things to the surface in an effort to help and heal itself for a better tomorrow. It's important to know the difference between what needs to be resurrected in your life and what needs to stay buried. By spiritually developing a sense of timing and propriety, under the anointing of the Holy Spirit you will be able to know what to do and say, and what not to do and say, concerning your past, present, and future. You must begin to see your life as a whole entity and accept it for what it is. Complaining about the circumstances of your life is a waste of time. Your progress is slowed through the pointlessness of regret. There is great victory in saying with the Apostle Paul, *"But by the grace of God I am what I am . . ." (1 Corinthians 15:10).*

Your past serves an important purpose, and that purpose is to reveal the *real* you. You were chosen in Him before the foundation of the world and, since then, He has been working all things together for the good of *that* person – the one who has encountered the process of life with all of its ups and downs. But spiritual time-travel allows you to live outside of the narrow-minded paradigm of disappointment. In rethinking your past, your previous disappointments will be transformed into important stepping-stones on the path to wholeness. The answers to your questions in the now can be found somewhere in your past or in your future, and the mobility of your spirit enables you to find the answers that you need for the "saving" of your soul. Activate your spirituality so that you can travel intelligently. Pray in the Spirit. Meditate God's Word. Maintain a good confession. Walk in faith. Think out of the box.

Keep talking yourself into your future. Your faith will propel you, like the Syrophoenician woman, into your own personal promised land of tomorrow. Maintain your motivation by staying mentally mobile. You can't afford to get your life stuck in a time warp now, because you know too much and there is too much for you to do. The future is calling you, so you must move forward! You're not getting older, but you *are* getting better as you grow in God and learn your life-lessons. Now is the time to embrace the sage-like wisdom and oak-like strength that comes from having lived a full life. When you learn how to successfully travel through time, and how all the parts of your life work together for good, you will be able to release any shame or regret that you have about yesterday, as well as any apprehension and/or anxiety that you may have about tomorrow. And now, fellow time-travelers, it's on to Chapter Two.

Meditations for Chapter One

1.

He has made everything beautiful in its TIME. He also has planted eternity in men's hearts and minds [a divinely implanted sense of a purpose working through the ages which nothing under the sun but only God, can satisfy], yet so that man cannot find out what God has done from the beginning to the end.
(Ecclesiastes 3:11 AMP)

2.

That which is now already has been, and that which is to be already has been; and God seeks that which has passed by [so that history repeats itself].
(Ecclesiastes 3:15 AMP)

3.

. . . The race is not to the swift, nor the battle to the strong, nor bread to the wise, nor riches to men of understanding, nor favor to men of skill; but TIME and chance happen to them all. (Ecclesiastes 9:11)

4.

For the vision is yet for an appointed TIME . . .
(Habakkuk 2:3)

5.

Then He said to her, "For this saying go your way; the demon has gone out of your daughter." And when she had come to her house, she found the demon gone out, and her daughter lying on the bed. (Mark 7:29, 30)

6.

But, beloved, do not forget this one thing, that with the Lord one day is as a thousand years, and a thousand years as one day. (2 Peter 3:8)

7.

. . . of the sons of Issachar who had UNDERSTANDING OF THE TIMES, to know what Israel ought to do . . . (1 Chronicles 12:32)

Chapter Two

The Whole Truth, and Nothing but the Truth

We know that God is always at work for the good of everyone who loves Him. They are the ones God has chosen for His purpose.
Romans 8:28 – Contemporary English Version

> Colonel Jessep (Jack Nicholson): You want answers?
> Kaffee (Tom Cruise): I want the truth!
> Jessep: You can't handle the truth!
> – from *A Few Good Men*

There is great freedom that comes by taking steps toward facing the whole truth about your life. If you live in denial about your past, or if you refuse to try to develop a plan for your future because you are ignoring the inevitability of it, you will not be able to assess your present situation honestly or realistically. Refusing to take responsibility for your life choices, blaming others for your mistakes, avoiding the admission of ownership of the reasons why your life is what it is – these things will blind you to the truth. Basically, they are the ways that you lie to yourself and, if you continually lie to yourself about your life, you will never be able to see how God is working everything in it together for your ultimate good. God dwells in the light, and in the light, every lie is exposed. Only the truth can free you, and because the God Who declares the end from the beginning is on your side, you have nothing to fear about facing it.

The first, and most important, step is becoming completely honest with Him about your *whole* life. God is good, and His mercy endures forever. Nothing can separate you from His love. You didn't do anything to obtain it, so you can't do anything that would cause you to lose it. The secret place of the Most High is and always will be a safe place for you and *your* secrets. Don't be afraid to tell Him *everything* about yourself – the good, the bad and the ugly. You have a High Priest Who empathizes with your weaknesses, and already knows you better than you know yourself, so you can remain fearlessly naked before Him when He comes to walk with you in the cool of the day. You don't ever have to scramble through your garden in a panic, frantically searching for religious or emotional "fig leaves" with which to hide yourself. He loves you unconditionally, so you don't have to protect yourself from His eyes.

The next step is becoming honest with yourself. You must live by faith, but faith is not denial. As a primarily spiritual being, you have to believe in the supernatural intervention of God in your affairs, without falling out of touch with reality about yourself. It is possible to remain perfectly positive about your life, while totally parting with any illusions concerning it. Jesus told His disciples that the Spirit of Truth would lead them into *all* the truth (John 16:13), and all means *all*. For you, personally, that includes all the truth about yourself – your origins, your ancestry, your history, your virtues and character flaws, everything about yourself that you are proud of, and everything that causes you shame. But the Spirit of Truth is also the Comforter, so you don't have to fear or dread looking deeply into your reality. You will gladly welcome the truth into your life when you begin to enjoy the taste of freedom that it brings.

Then, you must tell your truth to the people around you to complete the process. Now this part is a little tricky and requires real intelligence, great sensitivity, and absolute discretion. You see, when you are honest with God – even *completely* honest – you never run the risk of losing His unconditional love. And when you are truthful with yourself, you are never in danger of abandonment, because you are eternally connected to yourself, even if you *don't* love yourself unconditionally. But telling and living the truth before the people in your world is potentially dangerous. Even those who love you (or *think* they love you) the most, actually love the *image* of you that they hold in their minds. And if that image is threatened by a discovered discrepancy between it and the truth, most people will instinctively attempt to preserve and protect the *image* out of comfort-zone loyalty, and the consequences could be very negative.

In my last book, *Keepin' It Real,* I went into great detail about the importance of living an authentic life, regardless of the risk. I believe in the message of that book *now* even more than I did when I wrote it and sincerely recommend that you read it (even though it is theologically controversial) if you have a heart for living truthfully. The theme of *this* book, however, is quite different from that one, so I will not repeat what I've already said then and there. The point I'm making *here* is that all things, past, present and future, work together for good, but the past cannot work for you positively until you tell the undeniable truth about it. I'm not talking about blabbing to anyone and everyone the sordid details of every sin or transgression that you've ever committed. What's under the blood of Jesus needs to *stay* under the blood of Jesus. But you can and should be truthful about your *past* with God, yourself and others.

Just the Facts, Ma'am.

Telling the whole truth, and nothing but the truth, means being unpretentiously straightforward when talking about your roots, background, history, and ancestry. You can't know where you are going until you fully grasp where you've come from. It is certainly important to try to become the best version of yourself that you *can* become, but being the best "you" doesn't require the compromise of your true identity or the sacrifice of your real self. Never be embarrassed about your history or your relatives or your past relationships. They are all a part of you, whether you want to realize it or not, and have helped to shape you into who you now are, for good or for bad. Embrace the realities of your life and celebrate them, no matter how mundane or unglamorous or even painful that they may be. Maturity is evident in your life when you can begin to accept it as it is, and as it has been, up to this point.

I don't mean to offend any family members by this, but when I was growing up, I resented the fact that my name was Jimmy Earl. I was named after my father, Jimmy Swilley (the birth certificate reads "Jimmy," not James), and my uncle, Earl Paulk. To differentiate between my father and me, I was called by *both* names my whole life, and I never liked it. In a world of Billy Bobs, Jim Bobs, and other two-part monikers, I always felt that the name sounded too southern (country), too immature, and too unlike *me*! I thought that I should have a cooler, stronger, more modern-sounding name. But we are who we are, and my name is, and always will be, Jimmy Earl. We all have to deal with things about our lives that we don't like so much, so I have made peace with the name that was given me. And the fact is, I *am* southern, so I might as well have a southern sounding name. In all of our lives, the facts *are* the facts.

I also have had ambivalent feelings about the *significance* of being named for two very different men in my life. My dad, a good man who has faithfully served in the ministry his whole life, is as unlike me as he could possibly be. We have not always had a great relationship due to the communication challenges presented by our extreme differences. But at this point in both of our lives, we have grown to respect and appreciate each other for who we are, and I admire him for being the honorable person that he is. My uncle is a well-known and influential leader in the church who, despite the remarkable success that he has enjoyed and the amazing revelation in which he has walked, has been surrounded by controversy and scandal for as long as I can remember. Being linked to him has closed as many doors for me as it has opened, but I honor him "for the work's sake" and continue to go by my two names.

The impacting presence and influence of *both* men for whom I am named are the facts of my life. As I said before, the facts are the facts, whether we like them or not. A great many of them exist beyond our control, so we have no choice but to be proactive and to find a way to live peaceably with them. As a matter of fact, our lives are made up of *endless* facts – where we were born, to whom we were related, where we went to school, who we married, what we chose for an occupation, phone numbers, addresses, zip codes, social security numbers – a seemingly infinite number of statistics and significant calendar dates. And the longer we live, the more facts we collect and the harder it becomes to keep up with them all. But all the facts that we could ever collect won't reveal the essence of our lives. It is entirely possible to know all of the facts pertaining to someone's existence and not really know *them* at all.

The bottom line is that the *facts* of your life are not necessarily relevant to the *truth* of your life. Maya Angelou said, "There is a world of difference between facts and truth. Facts can obscure truth." Maybe we should all stop being so preoccupied with the facts, so that we can effectively search for the truth without unnecessary distraction. Jesus didn't say, "You shall know the *facts*, and the *facts* shall set you free;" He said "you shall know the *truth*!" And at the end of the day, it doesn't really matter so much what has or hasn't happened to you, or what your name is, or where you came from. What matters is who you *are* and how well you have played the hand that life dealt you. And yet, God *does* incorporate the facts of your life into His overall plan for your good, so it really *is* all good! Therefore, you can feel free to speak the truth about your past, your present, and what you want to happen in your future.

Confidence in Christ

Jesus said to him, "I am the . . . truth . . ."
                                                    – John 14:6

"Where is there dignity unless there is honesty?" – Cicero. Self-respect comes from knowing that you are living honestly, without compromise. If you sincerely believe that all things are working together for your good, you will want to bring all things to the table and lay them all out before the Lord. Maybe He will supply you with the answers to all of your questions, but probably not. Most of the answers are revealed through the process of time. The good news is, when you review your life, you don't *have* to understand why everything has happened the way that it has. You can trust God *without* having all the answers, because you know that He is good. Your life is still a work in progress and there are some mysteries that will not be solved until much closer to story's end. But those things that you *do* understand should be spoken of with candor. In the words of Mark Twain: "When in doubt, tell the truth."

People who walk in truth are confident people, confident enough to be willing to sacrifice acceptance and praise from others, if necessary. There is a certain confidence that only comes from knowing who you are in Christ. When you know that He has made you righteous and that He wants you to be involved with His plan of redemption for the earth, you begin to walk in a certain confidence that no one can give you and no one can take away from you. Righteousness consciousness means that your heart does not condemn you, and so it produces unshakable strength of character. Having confidence before God enables you to be confident before the world so that you can rise above any sense of inadequacy that could potentially paralyze you emotionally. Without this kind of confidence, it is possible to develop phony feelings of inferiority that come from comparing your life to the lives of others.

Ultimately, and most importantly, *Christ* is truth, and Christ is *your* truth. He is the Lord of your past life, your present life, and your future life. He is not a man that He should lie, and you can be sure that He will never lie to *you*. If God were to lie, everything in the universe as we know it would encounter an instant meltdown, because it is all held together by the word of His power. Everything is initially based on His truth. All life emanates from the truth of God. We all live by every word that proceeds from His mouth. And every *wrong* thing in the universe, and every *wrong* thing in your life, is the result of a perversion of God's truth – a rejection of His integrity – a disconnection from faith in His perfect Word. But the wrong can be made right, and the crooked places can be made straight. The truth heals. The truth restores. The truth blesses. The truth transcends. It reveals Christ in you, the Hope of Glory.

Meditations for Chapter Two

1.
Then Jesus turned to the Jews who had claimed to believe in Him. "If you stick with this, living out what I tell you, you are my disciples for sure. Then you will experience for yourselves the truth, and the truth will free you." (John 8:31, 32 The Message)

2.
So if the Son sets you free, you are free through and through. (John 8:36 The Message)

3.
Now the Lord is the Spirit; and where the Spirit of the Lord is, there is liberty. (2 Corinthians 3:17)

4.
And there is no creature hidden from His sight, but all things are naked and open to the eyes of Him to whom we must give account. (Hebrews 4:13)

5.
For we do not have a High Priest Who is unable to understand and sympathize and have a shared feeling with our weaknesses and infirmities and liability to the assaults of temptation, but One Who has been tempted in every respect as we are, yet without sinning. (Hebrews 4:15 AMP)

6.

*And thus the secrets of his heart are revealed; and so,
falling down on his face, he will worship God and report
that God is truly among you. (1 Corinthians 14:25)*

7.

*Put Me in remembrance [remind Me of your merits]; let
us plead and argue together. Set forth your case that you
may be justified (proved right). (Isaiah 43:26 AMP)*

Chapter Three

Healing Old Wounds

And we know that God causes all things to work together
for good to those who love God, to those who are called
according to His purpose.
Romans 8:28 – New American Standard Bible

Never let yesterday use up today.
— Richard H. Nelson

Self-pity keeps your old wounds alive. When you allow extreme sorrow for your own troubles to exist in your heart, and never attempt to rid it from your consciousness by looking for the possible positive, you inevitably create fertile emotional ground for the growth of negative strongholds in your life. Reinforced with bitterness, these strongholds eventually stifle your ability to travel successfully into your future, because, as you progress through your life and continue to collect offenses, you gradually slow your inner self down to a grinding halt. Unhealed wounds are guaranteed to evolve into time-warps, which are imaginary distortions of space in relation to time. They dam up the river of creativity and make your world smaller and smaller until you are spiritually suffocated and basically cease to exist on many levels. The damage you do to yourself becomes a cancer that eats away at your soul.

Time heals all wounds, unless you pick at them. At some point, you just have to make the decision to stop talking about the hurt and trauma that you have experienced and begin to focus on the good that has come from the pain. The more you try to extract pity from others, the more you seal your fate as a victim – and victims are prisoners, incarcerated by their own selfishness. Whether or not you are justified in your accusations, the point is that in the big picture, it really doesn't matter who did what, or who said what, or who didn't do what they were supposed to do, according to the script existing in your head. What matters is what you have *learned* from each experience, including the negative ones. You must train your mind to automatically look for the silver lining to every cloud in your personal sky until you can actually begin to see the beauty in every emotional scar and the sacredness of each spiritual wound.

David showed that he had grasped this concept when he said, *"It is good for me that I have been afflicted, that I may learn Your statutes" (Psalm 119:71)*. This really was an extraordinary thing for a man like David to say, because his warrior-like nature was wholly resistant to the embracing of affliction. But, through the process of time, we can see that David was not just *humbled* by the harsh realities of his life – he was actually *enlightened* by them, and this enlightenment built within him a remarkable inner strength. Improvement through affliction should be the goal for *every* wounded warrior, because, even though humility is an admirable virtue, it is not all-sufficient for the lives of those who are called according to His purpose. Humility buttressed by acquired wisdom, however, creates a certain kind of sober strength and mature confidence that causes a person to come to terms with his/her emotional wounds.

And you must always bear in mind that coming to terms with your emotional wounds and scars does not necessarily guarantee change in your *external* world. A more realistic expectation is that it will change your *perception* of things external by revising the internal map of memory and then, perhaps, the internal will bring change in the material realm from the inside out. For example, forgiveness does not always lead to a healed relationship. It can certainly bring healing to your *soul*, and enlightenment to your *mind* concerning the truth of a situation, but it might not ever change the person who wounded you. The bitter reality of relationships is that some people apparently are just not capable of love – or at least of *showing* love the way that you need for them to – so you have to let them go, along with your hurt and anger. The most important thing is that you find a way to benefit from the whole experience.

A Balm in Gilead

Is there no balm in Gilead, is there no physician there? Why then is there no recovery for the health of the daughter of my people?

Jeremiah 8:22

Gilead is the name used to indicate Israel's possession east of the Jordan River. It extended from the lower end of the Sea of Galilee to the northern end of the Dead Sea, and from the Jordan eastward to the desert, a plateau of some 2,000 feet elevation. At the time of Moses, it was a lush region with abundant forests, rich grazing lands, and plenty of moisture. The region became famous because of some of its products, particularly the balm that was exported to Tyre from Palestine (Ezekiel 27:17), an odoriferous resin obtained only in Gilead (Genesis 37:25; Jeremiah 46:11). It was used as an ointment for healing wounds (Jeremiah 51:8) and came from a small tree no longer found in Gilead. Jeremiah knew of its curative power and referred to it three times in the Scriptures. This "balm in Gilead" is a type of the comforting help of the Holy Spirit – the healing power that comes from heaven to save the souls of the emotionally wounded.

In Exodus 15:26, God refers to Himself as "the Lord who heals," a title that is translated from the Hebrew *Jehovah-Ropheka,* or *Jehovah-Rapha.* In this context, He speaks of *physical* healing as He promises that none of the plagues of the Egyptians would come on His covenant people. And, certainly, God *is* a healer of His physical creation, a fact that was confirmed in the atonement that was paid for by the horrible stripes that Jesus took for us all on His own tortured body. But one of the shades of interpretation of the term *Jehovah-Rapha* is literally *"the God who makes bitter experiences sweet,"* which implies that He is a healer for the inner man, as well as for the outer man. The balm in Gilead, therefore, is the working together of all things for the good of those who love God. The *good* that potentially comes from bitter experiences brings healing and restoration. It overcomes the evil. It heals the hurt and the pain.

"The lamp of the body is the eye. If therefore your eye is good, your whole body will be full of light" (Matthew 6:22). Jesus said these powerful words in His historical sermon on the mount. His meaning here was clear as He explained how *perception* – the way that you "see" your situation – determines the amount of light that you will contain in your body. The light, or illumination, concerning a thing that has happened to you will literally affect your physical well-being. Your outer man will respond to the light that you have inwardly. The light brings health, burning out the infection of bitterness and self-pity. The Holy Spirit is the Spirit of Understanding (Isaiah 11:2), and He applies the healing balm to the eyes of your soul, so that you can see clearly and can begin to finally *understand* how Jehovah-Rapha is making your bitter experiences sweet. Gilead's balm is an eye salve with miraculous and holistic properties.

The healing of old wounds enables you to break debilitating ties with the past, so that you can begin to see the beauty that now surrounds you. No longer blinded by the selfishness that forces you to walk through life facing backwards, you can see the path to a brighter future, where you no longer are compelled to make a case for holding grudges and nursing past offenses. By walking in the light you are enabled to just let it all go, no longer needing apologies and explanations – no longer stunted in your personal growth. David also said, *"I would have lost heart, unless I had believed that I would see the goodness of the Lord in the land of the living" (Psalm 27:13).* You *can* see the goodness of the Lord, and claim your citizenship in the land of the living, by choosing to walk in emotional and spiritual health. You don't have to remain in a perpetually wounded state, because there *is* a balm in Gilead for you!

That was Then; This is Now

When the Lord brought back the captives [who returned]
to Zion, we were like those who dream [it seemed so
unreal].
                                        Psalm 126:1 – AMP

A major factor in the healing of old wounds is the renewing of
the mind – changing the way that you think about the past and the
present. Repentance is the way into the Kingdom of God, and it
simply means to change your mind. Repentance is a basic concept
that is complex in its execution. It is possible and necessary, but
certainly not easy or immediate, because your survival instincts
have helped you to develop a way of co-existing with your
internal wounds. The methods by which you have devised a plan
of protection for your inner self are so much a part of the way
that you think and act and feel and move, that learning to live in a
healed state can be daunting and disorienting for you. Your long-
existing, unhealed wounds are not so much like old friends as they
are like close members of a severely dysfunctional family. You
actually hate them, but they are a part of you, and you are very
accustomed to their presence.

Learning to *think* a new way is like learning to *live* a new way. A true
lifestyle change requires the embracing of a whole new language
that is unfamiliar to your own ears, and sometimes difficult to
grasp. Breaking old patterns of self-defeating talk and negative
attitudes is a huge undertaking and one that many people find too
overwhelming. Mind renewal must be deliberate and constantly
reinforced. To rethink your personal life, you must continually
remind yourself that what happened in the past does not determine
what is happening now. The clock in your brain must be reset
many times before you actually begin to believe that things have
changed and that the internal wounds that once dominated your
life have truly lost their prominence and preeminence. You do
not deny their existence, but you *do* deny their authority over your
life. You are the redeemed of the Lord, and so *you* have the say-
so!

Mind renewal requires healing prayer, meditation in the Word, and discipline in your speech. It also may have to involve the intentional disconnection from negative people in your life, because some co-dependent relationships are based in unhealthy bonding around shared-wound experiences. Like sharks drawn to blood, the unhealed seek out others like themselves and build relationships on a corrupt foundation. Renewing your mind may cause you to re-evaluate your counter-productive relationships and ultimately cause you to fall out of fellowship with those who keep you bound to your past and prevent your emotional healing. You can't afford to let the fear of loneliness keep you from breaking off bad alliances. Disconnecting from negative people may inevitably catapult you into unfamiliar emotional territory, but in the land of the unfamiliar you are much less vulnerable to the "familiar spirits" of your past.

When you are healed, you no longer have to tolerate long-established feelings of low self-esteem, and you no longer feel compelled to tear yourself down verbally. Because you cease to feel inferior to others or threatened by them, you can free yourself from jealousy and resentment and can sincerely rejoice when they do well or when they have more than you. When you are healed, you can relax and really be yourself, without an unrealistic need for the approval of others. You can feel comfortably justified in loving yourself and can forgive yourself by accepting your own limitations, acknowledging them without apology. Most importantly, when you are healed, you can become a healer for others – an asset to the Kingdom of God. You can say, with conviction and authority, that all things really do work together for good to those who love God. Remembering your wounds, you can still say, **"It's all good!"**

Meditations for Chapter Three

1.
*The Lord is near to those who have a broken heart, and
saves such as have a contrite spirit. (Psalm 34:18)*

2.
*The sacrifices of God are a broken spirit, a broken and a
contrite heart – These, O God, You will not despise.
(Psalm 51:17)*

3.
*He heals the brokenhearted and binds up their wounds.
(Psalm 147:3)*

4.
*Surely He has borne our griefs and carried our sorrows;
Yet we esteemed Him stricken, smitten by God,
and afflicted. (Isaiah 53:4)*

5.
*For thus says the High and Lofty One Who inhabits
eternity, whose name is Holy: "I dwell in the high and
holy place with him who has a contrite and humble
spirit, to revive the spirit of the humble, and to revive the
heart of the contrite ones." (Isaiah 57:15)*

6.
*The Spirit of the Lord God is upon Me, because the Lord
has anointed Me to preach good tidings to the poor;
He has sent Me to heal the brokenhearted, to proclaim
liberty to the captives, and the opening of the prison to
those who are bound. (Isaiah 61:1)*

7.
*A bruised reed He will not break, And smoking flax
He will not quench . . . (Matthew 12:20)*

Chapter Four

Let Yesterday Go

And we know that in all things God works for the good of those who love Him, who have been called according to His purpose.
Romans 8:28 – New International Version

Finish each day and be done with it. Some blunders and absurdities no doubt crept in; forget them as soon as you can. Tomorrow is a new day; begin it well and serenely and with too high a spirit to be encumbered with your old nonsense.

– Ralph Waldo Emerson

The foundational theme of my ministry – in fact, my life's message – can be summed up in this one sentence: *God is always in the now and, therefore, to know Him, we must also live in the now.* This statement can be found, in some form, in every sermon that I preach and every book that I write. So I want to take this opportunity to say something I meant to say (and should have said) in the introduction to my devotional *A Year In The Now!* During the time of its writing, there were at least two or three popular secular books on the market about living in the now or about understanding the power of the present. I'm sure that they are great books, but I have made it a point to deliberately avoid reading any part of them, even though several people have given me copies of each of them. It is important to me to know that what I teach about the now comes purely from my own gift of revelation knowledge.

That being said, I also want to point out that this book must be read with a certain kind of spiritual insight, or its theme will come across as sounding contradictory to you. On the one hand, I am telling you here that your past, present and future should be integrated to give you a sense of your *whole* life and how God has been working all things together for your good through it *all*. But I am also telling you that you have to let the past go, so that you can live in the now. To the natural ear, these points can sound completely at odds with one another. You must hear what I am saying by the Spirit to be able to understand and discern how both of these truths can co-exist and how they can relate to you. This, then, is the mystery of it all: the past must be *embraced*, and the past must be *abandoned* . . . the past is your *friend*, and the past is your *enemy* . . . you must live your *whole life,* but you must live in the *now.*

Many people find it quite difficult to mentally balance such complex concepts. For example, my preaching has a very strong emphasis on grace and on the realities of who we are in Christ. But there are those who hear my message and do not have the maturity to understand that, even though we *are* forgiven and righteous in Him, there are still consequences for our actions. Jesus was wounded for our transgressions, but the way of the transgressor is still hard. I do believe that God laid the iniquity of us all on Christ and that the full extent of His wrath has been poured out on the cross. But if you commit a sin that causes you to break the *"law"* (stealing, violence, murder, etc.), you are still going to have to pay your debt to society. That debt must be paid, even though the *sin*-debt has been abolished on Jesus' cross. Paul said it this way: *"All things are lawful for me, but all things are not helpful . . ." (1 Corinthians 6:12).*

Committing adultery will not send you to hell, but it certainly can ruin your marriage, and even your life. Spiritual leaders who are exposed as having moral trouble do not lose their anointing, but they usually do lose their credibility and, thus, their ability to effectively influence their followers. Drinking alcohol will not cause you to lose your salvation, but getting arrested for a DUI can present some really serious personal and legal problems for you. My point here is that the sin problem has been settled in heaven, but it definitely has not been settled on the earth, so we, of necessity, are compelled to preach the dual messages of grace *and* holiness – righteousness *and* responsibility – without any sense of conflict or contradiction. In the same way, we must preach the importance of harmonizing the past with the present and future, as well as the fact that it is imperative to let the past go. **It's *all* good**.

"Oh, I Believe in Yesterday"

Paul McCartney's lyric in the classic, *Yesterday,* reflects a longing that we all can probably relate to on some level. The sense of loss, the pain of regret, and the need to come to terms with a failed relationship, causes a person to wish he/she could just turn back the hands of time to when everything seemed to be all right. How many times have you replayed a certain conversation in your head, wishing that you could edit the whole thing so that you could say what you *should* have said – or could delete what you *shouldn't* have said. But it's too late now. You can't take anything back. You can't change a single word. What's done is done, what has been said has been said, and there's no getting back to yesterday. And, even though time can be a great healer, the longer you leave a thing the way that it was, the more it becomes indelibly set in stone. You begin to believe in yesterday just because of its inevitable reality.

The past is the one thing in your life that you have absolutely no ability to change. No matter how much you talk about it, it is what it is (and it was what it was). The only thing you *can* change, as has already been said here, is your perception of the past. The things in your past that needed to be buried probably need to *stay* buried, because no matter how many times you dig them up to look at them, like a long-dead corpse, they still look the same, or worse. Your temptation to live in denial fosters a false sense of optimism that makes you think that if you unearth a thing to look at it again, it might not look so bad this time. The irrational voices in your head tell you that maybe the abuse wasn't as bad as you remember, or that maybe you terminated that destructive relationship prematurely. Like the Israelites in the wilderness, your revisionist view of Egypt makes you want to return there. Soon, you are moving in reverse.

But changing your perception of the past does not require you to lose your grip on reality. Growing up in a dysfunctional family probably was every bit as horrible as you remember that it was. It's not necessary to try to convince yourself otherwise. But you *can* look back with eyes of compassion on those who hurt you or failed you, learn from their mistakes, be thankful that that part of your life is over, and move on from it. Yes, it was bad – get over it. Yes, the people in your life made mistakes – forgive them anyway. Yes, you messed up – pick yourself up and get back to living your life. Yes, you have been slighted and used – remember that you're not perfect either, and you've hurt some people along the way, so give those who have hurt you a break. Maybe they're really sorry for what they did and, then again, maybe they don't even *realize* what they did. In either case, what really matters is where you are *now*.

". . . Father, forgive them, for they do not know what they do . . ." *(Luke 23:34)*. Praying these words that Jesus spoke before He died on the cross can be enormously helpful in the process of letting yesterday go. When you get to the point that you are able to actually pray for your enemies, you will discover that it gives you a great sense of emotional empowerment to do so. Forgiveness breaks the negative ties with the past and enables you to look back on what has happened to you with much more objectivity. When you distance yourself emotionally from your history, you can begin to tell yourself the truth about your past, and the truth, no matter how painful, is the only path to freedom. Believe in yesterday, but only in the sense that you are thankful for having experienced and *survived* it. Learn your lessons well, so that you can avoid making the same mistakes again and can turn the course of your life in the right direction.

God in the Now

Every day that I live, I fall in love with the idea of knowing God in the now more than I did the previous day. The whole concept of eternity and timelessness and being able to start over with a clean slate – every bit of it – just makes me really happy on the inside. Even though some people still don't understand why we named our church "Church In The Now," I've never once second-guessed the decision to do so. Each day that I drive onto our church property and see the towering sign overlooking Interstate 20 that displays the church name in big yellow letters, I rejoice in the whole idea of it all over again. Others may think that the sign, with its purple neon and extreme height, is a little over the top, and even a bit gaudy, but to me it looks like an enormous gate that opens up into another dimension. In my view, the message of "now" is so big, that it can't be displayed in an unassuming, understated medium.

It is with the same passion that I declare to you as you read these pages, that you really can live in the now and can experience all the hope and possibilities that come with that truth. I urge you, with everything in me, to let yesterday go. Who or what is binding you to your past? Who can't you forgive? Who is keeping you from moving into the now? Nobody, and I mean *nobody,* is worth losing your destiny over! What event in your life has stopped your progression? What heartbreak or trauma arrested your development? Nothing, and I mean *nothing,* is worth causing you to miss your path of purpose! I'm not denying the severity of what may have happened to you in the past, nor am I trying to justify anyone or anything. And maybe you're not ready to hear someone tell you to get over it, but I do hope you see that your life is bigger than the people whom you have known or the things that you have experienced.

You *can* get past the pain. You *can* renew your mind. You *can* rethink your history. You *can* break old patterns, mindsets, and habits. You *can* pull down negative strongholds. You *can* end a generational curse. You *can* create a better future for your children.

You *can* find it in your heart to forgive. You *can* forgive yourself. You *can* turn your weaknesses into strengths. You *can* learn from your mistakes and not repeat them. You *can* start over. You *can* find the grace that you need to deal with a seemingly impossible situation. You *can* make peace with your past and then give it a proper burial. You *can* develop a realistically positive outlook. You *can* find redemption in a relationship that has turned ugly. You *can* rise above it all. You *can* grow through hardships. You *can* feel confident about your life. You *can* trust in your ability to make good decisions. You *can* stop punishing yourself. You *can* really believe again.

Letting yesterday go means living in the now, and living in the now means believing that all things really are possible. Letting yesterday go is a celebration of the mercies of God that are new every morning. Letting yesterday go is making a declaration to yourself that you can rejoice in the day that the Lord has made, no matter what circumstances may occur during that day. Letting yesterday go is acknowledging that to everything there is a season, and then discerning when your season has changed. Letting yesterday go is trusting God and being willing to follow Him into uncharted territory. It means never saying "never." It means keeping an open mind and being aware of all your options. It means realizing that *every* day God sets before you life and death, blessing and cursing, and that you have the ability to *choose* life and blessing. Letting yesterday go is focusing on what you have in your hand right now.

Meditations for Chapter Four

1.

I'm not saying that I have this all together, that I have it made. But I am well on my way, reaching out for Christ, who has so wondrously reached out for me. Friends, don't get me wrong: By no means do I count myself an expert in all of this, but I've got my eye on the goal, where God is beckoning us onward – to Jesus. I'm off

*and running, and I'm not turning back. So let's keep
focused on that goal, those of us who want everything
God has for us. If any of you have something else in
mind, something less than total commitment, God will
clear your blurred vision – you'll see it yet! Now that
we're on the right track, let's stay on it.
(Philippians 3:12-16 The Message)*

2.

*I didn't die. I lived! And now I'm telling the world what
God did. God tested me, He pushed me hard, but He
didn't hand me over to death. Swing wide the city gates
– the righteous gates! I'll walk right through and thank
God! This Temple Gate belongs to God, so the victors
can enter and praise. (Psalm 118:17-20 The Message)*

3.

*Now faith is the substance of things hoped for, the
evidence of things not seen. (Hebrews 11:1)*

4.

*But we all, with unveiled face, beholding as in a mirror
the glory of the Lord, are being transformed into the
same image from glory to glory, just as by the Spirit of
the Lord. (2 Corinthians 3:18)*

5.

*For a righteous man may fall seven times and rise again,
but the wicked shall fall by calamity.
(Proverbs 24:16)*

6.

*This is the day the LORD has made; we will rejoice and
be glad in it. (Psalm 118:24)*

7.

Remember Lot's wife. (Luke 17:32)

Chapter Five

Connecting the Dots and Finding Missing Pieces to the Puzzle

And we know that God causes everything to work together for the good of those who love God and are called according to His purpose for them.
Romans 8:28 – New Living Translation

> The universe is one great kindergarten for man. Everything that exists has brought with it its own peculiar lesson. The mountain teaches stability and grandeur; the ocean immensity and change. Forests, lakes, and rivers, clouds and winds, stars and flowers, stupendous glaciers and crystal snowflakes – every form of animate or inanimate existence, leaves its impress upon the soul of man.
>
> – Orison Swett Marden

There definitely is a pattern to your life – a big picture that God Himself has painted. It is up to you to keep looking intently at the artwork created from your personal circumstances, until the whole thing begins to make some sense to you. You probably have seen one of those "Magic Eye" images that is actually a picture within a picture. When you look at it initially, you can only see a colorful design, but as you continue to stare at the image, your eye eventually discovers the hidden picture concealed within the pattern. That picture was there all along, but you couldn't see it at first. Locating the plan for your life is much like that. Through a process of solving riddles, discerning the roles of significant people in your life, and learning to distinguish between random coincidences and meaningful events, you begin to see another image emerge from the background and gradually move into the foreground of your life.

God will certainly give you clues along the way to help you discover your hidden picture, but, whether you want to believe it or not, the biggest part of the unique plan for your life is revealed to you through your relationships with other people. We learn about our relationship with Him through parental, familial, and romantic relationships, as well as through our friendships and acquaintances. Some of the people in your life enter into the picture for a season, and some of them will be in or around your world indefinitely, but they all play a part and serve a purpose in revealing God's will for your life. To better make this point, I have divided the people in your life into seven categories. You may locate some of them in more than one of the categories, but they all are essential to the unfolding of your unique plan, and *you* must connect the dots and recognize the people who are the missing pieces to your puzzle.

1. Designers

The first group, I call the **designers**. These are the people who lay the foundation, initiate the patterns, and in many ways, set the boundaries of your life. The major players here are, of course, your parents, whether you were raised in a traditional, two-parent home, a blended family, or in a single-parent household. Even if you were adopted or raised in a foster home, your biological parents have affected you as much as your adoptive parents, I believe, because of the equal balance between *nature* and *nurture.* Physical DNA and family environment, together, serve to design who you are. Even if you never *knew* your parents, or never knew who they were, they are still a major factor in your destiny. Even if you were orphaned at an early age, your biology is, just the same, a very strong force in your life. Your 46 chromosomes are exactly 23 from your biological mother, plus 23 from your biological father.

2. Developers

The next group, I refer to as the **developers.** This category is comprised of those people who were significant early influences in your life – siblings, step-parents, playmates, teachers, etc. – and, in many ways, these people have affected you as dramatically as did your designers. Basically, you come into the world as a blank canvas, and your early relationships have the opportunity to paint on that canvas with the broadest of strokes. Early experiences, encounters and exchanges serve to build a world-view that can last your whole life long. The words spoken to you in your formative years still communicate to you, on some level, every day of your life, and the first things that you experienced paved emotional and psychological roads on which you still travel. Part of making peace with the past is trying to understand what happened in the genesis of your personal journey that set the tone for all the rest of your time-travel.

3. Depositors

The **depositors** are those people who have been sent to you for a specific purpose and with whom you have encountered a seasonal relationship. They are the ones who came to impart something singular to you, without developing any further dialogue in your life. These people are the ships that are *meant* to pass you in the night and are destined to continue to sail on. It is important to discern the role of the depositors and to know how much or how little to expect of them. They are not supposed to be in your life long-term. They are in another destiny and reality that is separate from yours, but they had something that you needed at a certain time and so they were sent into your world to make a special delivery. Depositors cannot be expected to be dependable for lasting relationships. Once they have fulfilled their unique purpose in the work of God for good, their season with you is over and they must exit the stage.

4. Deceivers

These "truth-testers" perform a necessary evil in your life. *Deceivers* are sent to you to put your truth on trial and without them you can never know what you *really* believe about God or about yourself. These are your tempters and accusers – the ones who appeal to your dark side and then reveal it for what it really is. Your personal strength can only be built by resolving to overcome them and by exposing the lies that they have tried to make you believe, by the way that you live out your life. You must prove the deceivers wrong. As Jesus "made an open show" of demonic principalities, you must demonstrate God's truth about yourself, in spite of what the deceptive influences have attempted to establish. Overcome that one who said that you were a loser *by winning.* Prevail over that one who called you a failure *by succeeding.* And don't waste your time trying to prove it to *them* – instead, prove the truth to *yourself.*

5. Destroyers

In Isaiah 54:16, God says that *He* has created the destroyer to destroy, but in verse 17, He says that no weapon formed against you would prosper. The *destroyers* are those who have been sent to potentially ruin your life. Whether these people were sent by God or the devil is a moot point. What matters is that you determine to overcome the evil with the good and, in so doing, you become stronger, not just *in spite* of the destroyers, but *because* of them! Joseph's brothers tried to be his destroyers but, instead, they became the means by which he ultimately became the ruler of Egypt and provided the way in which he was able to make his own dreams come true. By knowing how to respond proactively to possible destruction, you demonstrate that you truly are the head and not the tail, above only and not beneath. As cliché as it may sound, in fact, that which does not kill you really does make you stronger.

6. Deprogrammers

Deprogrammers are those wonderful people who help you to see things differently – the enablers that help you to obtain a positive paradigm shift. The man of integrity who comes into the life of a woman who has been previously abused by men, ultimately helps her to rethink the opposite sex for the better. The survivor of a horrible divorce who is able to be blessed with another chance at marital happiness finds himself wed to a deprogrammer who helps him develop a completely different view of marriage. That pastor who is a true shepherd becomes a deprogrammer for those wounded sheep who have been the victim of toxic church relationship experiences, and so it goes. There is someone out there who can help you change your mind – someone to help you face your fears, overcome your prejudices, and pull down your strongholds. These bearers of truth are sent to you to free you to find your destiny.

7. Definers

The key to connecting the dots and finding the missing pieces to your puzzle is determining to make all of the people in your life fit into the category of **definers** of your destiny. In making this a priority, you will cause things to begin to work together for your good. Proverbs says that relationships are like iron that sharpens iron and, if you can embrace that concept, then *all* of the people in your life – friends, family members, enemies, designers, developers, even destroyers – begin to serve a common purpose. They all are sent to you to help you define your destiny and perceive your purpose. In understanding that they are all necessary, you will become more tolerant of others and will be able to appreciate them in ways that you never would have thought possible. You can even enjoy the table that is spread for you in the presence of your enemies and give thanks for the bountiful feast that God Himself has provided.

Meditations for Chapter Five

1.

For no other foundation can anyone lay than that which is laid, which is Jesus Christ. (1 Corinthians 3:11)

2.

Whom will he teach knowledge? And whom will he make to understand the message? Those just weaned from milk? Those just drawn from the breasts? For precept must be upon precept, precept upon precept, line upon line, line upon line, here a little, there a little. (Isaiah 28:9, 10)

3.

To everything there is a season, a time for every purpose under heaven. (Ecclesiastes 3:1)

4.

Open rebuke is better than love carefully concealed. Faithful are the wounds of a friend, but the kisses of an enemy are deceitful. (Proverbs 27:5, 6)

5.

"Behold, I have created the blacksmith who blows the coals in the fire, who brings forth an instrument for his work; and I have created the spoiler [destroyer] to destroy. No weapon formed against you shall prosper, and every tongue which rises against you in judgment you shall condemn. This is the heritage of the servants of the Lord, and their righteousness is from Me," says the Lord. (Isaiah 54:16, 17)

6.

But, speaking the truth in love, may grow up in all things into Him Who is the head – Christ. (Ephesians 4:15)

7.

As iron sharpens iron, so a man sharpens the countenance of his friend. (Proverbs 27:17)

Chapter Six

No Regrets!

That's why we can be so sure that every detail in our
lives of love for God is worked into something good.
Romans 8:28 – The Message

I was regretting the past and fearing the future.
Suddenly my Lord was speaking: "My name is 'I
AM.' He paused. I waited. He continued, "When
you live in the past with its mistakes and regrets, it is
hard. I am not there. My name is not 'I WAS.'

When you live in the future, with its problems and
fears, it is hard. I am not there. My name is not 'I
WILL BE.'

When you live in this moment it is not hard. I am
here – My name is 'I AM.'"

– Helen Malicoat

"Brethren, I do not count myself to have apprehended; but
one thing I do, forgetting those things which are behind . . ."
(Philippians 3:13). The Apostle wrote these famous words to
the church, with the emphasis on the phrase *"one thing I do."*
The implication here is that moving past the past had become so
important to him that it had become the *one* thing – the *one*, top
priority – that he deemed necessary to live a successful life. Like
Paul, you *can* and *must* move past your temptation to be bound to
your past by regret. You *can* and *must* make the conscious effort
to forget those things that are behind you, knowing that the past
is the one thing that you cannot ever change. You are redeemed
from regret, because Jesus Christ has abolished the necessity for

sin-consciousness in His own body in the atonement. You can know that the negative past is forgotten and permanently lost in a mystical sea of mercy.

The forgiveness of God is a real thing. You can absolutely rest assured that He is faithful to His Word concerning the absolution of *all* of your sins – past, present and future – and that you were chosen, in Him, before the foundation of the world, to be holy and blameless before Him in love. Choose to walk in the *reality* of the fact that you *are* the righteousness of God in Christ. Glory in the cross and in the power of Jesus' blood, which is alive through the Eternal Spirit. Honor Him by refusing to feel guilty or oppressed over your past transgressions. Accept no charge from the accuser of the brethren, but demonstrate the triumph of grace by overcoming him by the blood of the Lamb (the part of your salvation that only *He* can supply) and by the word of your testimony (the part of your salvation that only *you* can supply). His mercies are new every morning, so think and act like you believe they are.

Remember that refusing to live in regret over your sins does not give you license to act irresponsibly, nor does it give you permission to live your life without conscience or conviction. But the recognition of the greatness of God's grace should *always* be a larger part of your life than should be any introspection, including godly sorrow. As we have already stated, the way of the transgressor *is* hard, but you can never underestimate the goodness and longsuffering of your merciful heavenly Father, the intercession of your ever-attentive Elder Brother/High Priest, nor the abiding present help of the Holy Spirit. God has not dealt with you after your sins, nor rewarded you according to your iniquities. Where your sin has abounded, His grace has much more abounded. There is therefore now no condemnation to you. When Jesus declared, "It is finished!" on the cross, He once and for all removed your need for regret.

You're Only Human

But what about the regret that you possess over the things that have or haven't happened with the *people* in your life? In the course of human events there is so much potential for pain and disappointment that you can be tempted to conclude that it would be better and easier to just live a completely isolated life. No relationship is perfect, and we have all failed in them and have all been the victim of the failure of others in the same way. But life goes on, and we certainly cannot survive without human contact, so we have to learn to relate without regret and to be thankful for what we have and for the fact that we are still loved in spite of our own imperfection. But living without regret is not living in denial. The fact is that some relationships in your life *are* irreparably damaged and there is simply nothing that can be done to change that reality. The important thing is to accept the truth and release the regret.

You must find the courage and walk in the integrity to take responsibility for your actions toward others. Claim full ownership to your *mistakes*, even though you know that you have been forgiven of your *sins*. Admit that you were wrong if you were, indeed, in the wrong. If possible, take appropriate action to rectify any and all situations where you may have acted dishonorably or have caused hurt or pain. But, after you have made the effort to right any of the wrongs that you may have committed, you must move on. You need to learn from your mistakes, but you don't need to dwell on them. Whether or not your attempt to fix the damage that you may have caused is *received*, the important thing is to know that you have at least made the effort and, *that* alone, must be sufficient for your peace of mind. God's forgiveness is guaranteed, so you can accept the forgiveness of others and then you can forgive yourself.

The Time is Now

Believing that all things are working together for your good prevents you from regretting any wasted time in your history, because you know that He will redeem that time and restore to you the very *years* that the pests ate away from your life. You must understand Jesus' parable of the miracle of the wage that was paid to those who came in at the eleventh hour – the one that was equivalent to that of those who had worked all day long. Put your name in that story and claim the truth of it for your very own. Because God transcends time, you can transcend it, as well. It is never too late for a miracle. It is not too late for you to fulfill your destiny. You don't need to lament over missed opportunities and wasted windows of time. The Lord of the now is also the God of a second chance, so there is no point in wasting your time regretting the time that you have already wasted! Grasp the now!

You will walk in great peace and contentment when you accept the fact that you are exactly where you need to be on your personal life-path. You don't have to be anxious about time. This peace of mind will ultimately cause you to become truly thankful in *everything*, believing that He is supernaturally perfecting that which concerns you by causing all things to work together for your good. You can rejoice that your own coat of many colors is woven with many different threads – threads of victory, defeat, joy, sorrow, triumph, failure, accomplishments and mistakes – and the finished product is a beautiful garment of praise that is uniquely tailor-made for you. When you eventually become comfortable wearing that coat – when it finally fits you – you will be able to confidently say that you wouldn't change a thing in your biography, and really mean it. Living without regret is truly the abundant life.

Meditations for Chapter Six

1.
But as for you, you meant evil against me; but God meant it for good, in order to bring it about as it is this day, to save many people alive. (Genesis 50:20)

2.
Blessed is he whose transgression is forgiven, whose sin is covered. Blessed is the man to whom the Lord does not impute iniquity, and in whose spirit there is no deceit. (Psalm 32:1, 2)

3.
For You, Lord, are good, and ready to forgive, and abundant in mercy to all those who call upon You. (Psalm 86:5)

4.
He who covers his sins will not prosper, but whoever confesses and forsakes them will have mercy. (Proverbs 28:13)

5.
Behold, it was for my peace that I had intense bitterness; but You have loved back my life from the pit of corruption and nothingness, for You have cast all my sins behind Your back. (Isaiah 38:17 AMP)

6.
I, even I, am He who blots out and cancels your transgressions, for My own sake, and I will not remember your sins. Put Me in remembrance [remind Me of your merits]; let us plead and argue together. Set forth your case, that you may be justified (proved right). (Isaiah 43:25, 26 AMP)

7.

*And when they had received it, they complained against
the land-owner, saying, "These last men have worked
only one hour, and you made them equal to us who have
borne the burden and the heat of the day." So the last
will be first, and the first last. For many are called, but
few chosen. (Matthew 20:11, 12, 16)*

Chapter Seven

Back to the Future: Rewriting Your History

We know that in everything God works for the good of those who love Him. They are the people He called, because that was His plan.

Romans 8:28 – New Century Version

> To keep our faces toward change, and behave like free spirits in the presence of fate, is strength undefeatable.
>
> – Helen Keller

In Chapter One, I discussed my lifelong interest in, and affection for, the concept of time travel. I referred there to Marty McFly, the character famously played by Michael J. Fox in the sci-fi comedy *Back To The Future*, and how that character had to return to the past to correct a problem in the present. Actually, the necessity for his time travel was about preserving his own *existence,* because, in the story, Marty had to go back in time to make sure that his parents would meet, so that he could be born. Spiritually, you may need to revisit and rethink some things in your past, taking dominion over them mentally and emotionally, so that they can begin to work together for the good of *your* existence. The longer I live, the more I realize that the working together of all things for good is not necessarily automatic and that we all need to do our part to make sure that the things in our lives really *do* work out for our benefit.

By developing your spiritual senses to see your whole life from God's perspective, you can essentially reinvent yourself, and, in a sense, rewrite your own history. Ultimately, you are who *He* says that you are, and you have been that person, in Him, from the foundation of the world. But *you* have the ability to self-create the best version of yourself by your own decrees and actions. It is possible for you to become the person that you have always wanted to be, because that desire was placed within you by God Himself. When you came to the knowledge of the Truth, you passed from death unto life and became a new creation, but in the larger sense, you are who you always have been. Even as you read this, you are the infant you, the current you, the elderly you, and, most importantly, the *eternal* you. You are in the now, so you should be in the process of bringing your *whole* consciousness into the now.

You may ask, "If I am who I always have been, how can I rewrite my history?" That's a very good question, and one that must be answered with spiritual insight. It is true that the past can't be changed, so to rewrite your history, you must embrace an *alternate* past reality. A classic example of this is found in the Genesis account of Sarah's response to God's promise that she would give birth in her old age. In chapter 18 it says that Sarah scoffingly laughed with unbelief at the word of the Lord (v. 12), that the Lord rebuked her for it (v. 13), and that she lied to the Lord about it out of fear (v. 15). Then, in chapter 21, after the birth of Isaac, Sarah puts a completely different spin on the fact that she laughed: *"And Sarah said, 'God has made me laugh, and all who hear will laugh with me'" (Genesis 21:6)*. She actually turned something negative into a positive, even naming her son "Isaac," which means *laughter*!

In the eleventh chapter of Hebrews, which is often referred to as "Faith's Hall of Fame," it is simply said of Sarah that she *"judged Him faithful Who had promised."* In fact, when you compare the Old Testament stories of Noah, Abraham, Moses, Samson, and David with how these men are presented in Hebrews 11, you see a lot of revisionist history. Each of these men made colossal blunders in their faith, yet in this chapter they are seen *only* as examples and heroes of faith. In the same way, when you compare the Old Testament Scriptures that Jesus quoted which are recorded in the Gospels, you see that He liberally claimed the license to quote them out of context, and make them say something quite different from their original meaning, for His own purposes. Many things about the language and tone of the New Testament seem to point to the fact that the past may not be as fixed and permanent as we might think.

The Revised Version

Rewriting your history begins by learning to love yourself unconditionally *now*. For example, you can and should hate your *sin nature*, but you must remember that *you* are not your *sin*. Hating your *sin* is right – hating *yourself* is wrong. In Romans 7:15-17, Paul makes this distinction clearly and candidly when he says, *"For what I am doing, I do not understand. For what I will do, that I do not practice; but what I hate, that I do. If, then, I do what I will not to do, I agree with the law that it is good. But now, it is no longer I who do it, but sin that dwells in me."* He shows here that he easily envisioned a discernable disconnection between *sin* and *self* and could therefore move on, in grace, to walk in the spirit. The same thing can be said for the mistakes that you have made in your life. Remember, *you* are not your mistakes, and *you* are not your bad behavior. *You* are not your poor life-choices. It is important for you to keep these things separate in your mind.

Rewriting your history also involves the continual letting go of your past failures. As necessary to personal growth as it is to own and embrace responsibility for yourself, at some point you have to stop hiding behind memories of failure and refuse to use them as excuses for mediocrity or lack of achievement. The past does not always dictate the future. You can grow and you can change for the better. Believing in yourself means giving yourself the benefit of the doubt, giving yourself another chance, and allowing your own possibilities and hidden potential to manifest. You must stop blaming yourself for everything that has gone wrong in your life. What has happened has happened. At some point it becomes counterproductive to try to place blame on *anyone* for *anything*. Jesus said that it was unimportant whether the boy was blind because he sinned, or because his parents did. Put things in perspective and move on.

Rewriting your history is learning from your mistakes, which is basically the same thing as befriending an old enemy. The well-beaten path of memory may be familiar, but it is not necessarily paved with concrete. It can be peaceably traveled, and even redirected, by the insight that comes from an enlightened paradigm shift. Revelation, understanding and forgiveness can reroute the old paths of self-destructive thinking and turn even the most negative memories into something completely different. The things that have been persistently painful and difficult to deal with can be converted into building blocks for a new road to a different and better future, if you are willing to look back through a new window. Old patterns *can* be broken. Negative strongholds *can* be pulled down. History *can* be changed to the point that is doesn't have to repeat itself. The shadow cast over the present and future by the past *can* dissolve.

Now Faith Is

With all of the hope presented by the revisionist history of the eleventh chapter of Hebrews, the best part of the passage is summed up in the first three words of it: *"Now faith is."* All of Chapter Fourteen of this book is dedicated to this powerful, amazing phrase, so I'll say more about it there. But the embracing of these three words is your ticket to progressive travel through the times of your life. On several occasions it is recorded in the Scriptures that *"the just shall live by faith,"* and I would like to submit to you that "the just" (literally "the justified ones") must live their past, present and future life *all* by faith! Faith is now, but it prevails over yesterday and tomorrow. Even the word *justified* is revisionist in nature, because it means, *"just as if I had never sinned."* God, through His mercy, allows us to have a different past than we have actually had, and that very same mercy is renewed for you every morning of your life!

Get a picture of who you want to be and where you want to be on your life-path. Develop a prophetic vision that will produce a hope-image to which your faith may give real substance. Lay down all of your impossibility thinking and dare to review your life with fresh vision – vision that is unclouded with self-pity or by victim mentality. By faith, pull down the psychological or intellectual prisons that you have built up over time – those things that continue to exalt themselves against the knowledge of God – and bring every thought captive to the obedience of Christ. Make the quality decision to line up your life with the proceeding word of God, and determine to be a doer of it, and not a hearer only, so that you do not deceive yourself on any level. Live the life for which God created you. Take responsibility. Take action. Take the right road. Take heart. You can start making necessary changes immediately.

Meditations for Chapter Seven

1.
The spirit of man [that factor in human personality
which proceeds immediately from God] is the lamp of
the Lord, searching all his innermost parts.
(Proverbs 20:27 AMP)

2.
Do not [earnestly] remember the former things; neither
consider the things of old. Behold, I am doing a new
thing! Now it springs forth; do you not perceive and
know it and will you not give heed to it? I will even
make a way in the wilderness and rivers in the desert.
(Isaiah 43:18, 19 AMP)

3.
Put Me in remembrance [remind Me of your merits]; let
us plead and argue together. Set forth your case that you
may be justified (proved right).
(Isaiah 43:26 AMP)

4.

And they shall rebuild the ancient ruins; they shall raise
up the former desolations and renew the ruined cities,
the devastations of many generations.
(Isaiah 61:4 AMP)

5.

For by [faith – trust and holy fervor born of faith] the
men of old had divine testimony borne to them and
obtained a good report. (Hebrews 11:2 AMP)

6.

But without faith it is impossible to please and be
satisfactory to Him. For whoever would come near to
God must [necessarily] believe that God exists and that
He is the Rewarder of those who earnestly and diligently
seek Him [out]. (Hebrews 11:6 AMP)

7.

Because of faith also Sarah herself received physical
power to conceive a child, even when she was long past
the age for it, because she considered [God] Who had
given her the promise to be reliable and trustworthy and
true to His word. (Hebrews 11:11 AMP)

SECTION TWO

PERCEIVING PURPOSE
IN YOUR PRESENT

Pursuing purpose in your
present is the second step
to successfully living your
whole life.

·T·O·D·A·Y·

°T° is for **This**. *This is the day the Lord has made; We will rejoice and be glad in it. (Psalm 118:24)*

> . . . perceive the meaning of the power of **"this"** – the thing that God has placed in your hand for such a time as **this** . . .

°O° is for **Opportunity**. *Therefore, as we have **opportunity**, let us do good to all, especially to those who are of the household of faith. (Galatians 6:10)*

> . . . perceive the purpose of the **opportunity**
> presently presented to you, and have the wisdom and boldness to take appropriate action . . .

°D° is for **Destiny**. *For whom He foreknew, He also pre**destined** to be conformed to the image of His Son, that He might be the firstborn among many brethren. (Romans 8:29)*

> . . . perceive the present reality of **destiny** unfolding right now.
> The things happening right now are important to the big picture;
> so don't hesitate to wholeheartedly seize the day . . .

°A° is for **Alpha**. *I am the **Alpha** and the Omega, the Beginning and the End," says the Lord, "who is and who was and who is to come, the Almighty. (Revelation 1:8)*

> . . . perceive that today is a new beginning for you,
> the **alpha** and genesis of a whole new dimension of
> understanding and manifestation . . .

°**Y**° is for **Yes!** *For all the promises of God in Him are **Yes**, and in Him Amen, to the glory of God through us. (2 Corinthians 1:20)*

. . . perceive the positive around you.
Life is saying "**yes**" to you in the now, so let go of every negative impulse, and live yours to the fullest . . .

There are many fine things which

you mean to do some day, under

what you think will be more

favorable circumstances.

But the only time that is yours is

the present.

— Grenville Kleiser

Chapter Eight

"This" and "That"

And we know, that to men that love God, all things work together into good, to them that after purpose be called saints.

Romans 8:28 – Wycliffe New Testament

> We have always held to the hope, the belief, the conviction that there is a better life, a better world, beyond the horizon.
>
> – Franklin D. Roosevelt

"This is my body . . ." (Luke 22:19)

So many people spend their lives looking for *that,* that they rarely, if ever, are able to see the miracle of *this.* Jesus, in serving the Passover Seder to His disciples, broke bread and said to them the astonishing words: *"THIS is my body."* He did not say "this *represents* my body," or "this *signifies* my body." He actually said this *IS* my body! Even though He had a physical body that they could see and touch, the *this* to which He referred was the bread that He held in His hands and *this* was also the assemblage of men around that table. *It* **and** *they* were His body! But *this* had another meaning, as well. In a sense, Jesus was saying that *this moment – this special event – this last meal* that we will share together, is also my body. In this respect, He was saying that the manifestation of His body is the *comprehension* and *appreciation* of the *now* – the seizing of the moment. Christ, the *I AM,* is in the now! Christ is *this!*

Jesus further told His disciples in the same breath to *"do THIS in remembrance of me."* Once again we see this little word take on yet another dimension in its meaning. The *this* to which He was referring here is the re-enactment – the recapturing, if you will – of "this moment in time." In Paul's restating of these words of Jesus in his first letter to the Corinthians, he added the phrase (concerning the wine): *"This do,* as often as you drink it, *in remembrance of Me."* Doing *this often* is an act of remembrance, and to "re-member" something means to put the members back together again. *Remember* is the opposite of *dismember,* so the reuniting or reassembling of the members of the Body of Christ is a *this* moment phenomenon. It is a supernatural thing that can only be accomplished *in the now,* because those original twelve men at the table can never be reassembled, as they were, in exactly the same way.

The original "last supper" is a thing of the past. It is a *that.* But when believers who comprehend the power of the bread and the wine unite, or *re-member* Christ's body with some level of revelation, it becomes a *this* – a *now* thing. Jesus said that where two or more are gathered together in His name, there He *is*! *He is this!* The writer of the book of Hebrews said that they who come to God must believe that He *is*! *He is this!* *"But the righteousness of faith speaks in this way, 'Do not say in your heart, "Who will ascend into heaven?" (that is, to bring Christ down from above) or, "Who will descend into the abyss?" (that is, to bring Christ up from the dead). But what does it say? 'The word is near you, in your mouth and in your heart' (that is, the word of faith which we preach.)" – Romans 10:6-8.* Christ is here because we say that He is here. He is here in us. We do *this* in remembrance of Him!

"But this is that which was spoken by the prophet Joel." (Acts 2:16 KJV)

On the day of Pentecost, Peter, in response to the accusation that those who had been filled with the Spirit in the upper room were drunk, chose an interesting phrase to connect the unprecedented events of the day with the words of an Old Testament prophet. Joel had prophesied centuries earlier that God would pour out

His Spirit on all flesh in the days of fulfillment. In describing this outpouring, he talked about sons and daughters prophesying, old men dreaming dreams, young men seeing visions, wonders in the heavens and in the earth like blood, fire, pillars of smoke, the sun turning dark, and the moon turning into blood. Basically, he described everything *but* 120 believers speaking in other languages that people from other countries could understand. When you compare the second chapter of Joel with the second chapter of Acts, you see virtually no similarity whatsoever, and yet Peter said that *this* was *that!*

Was Peter misinterpreting Scripture? Certainly not! As a matter of fact, I imagine that Peter, a fisherman by trade, was probably not all that familiar with the words of the prophets of old to begin with. And I think that it is safe to assume that he would not have had the theological expertise to find a connection with the *this* of what was happening in Jerusalem on that day, and the *that* of Joel's prophecy. But I do believe that he spoke these inspired words under the unction of the Holy Spirit. He was prophesying a *now* word and, most likely, had no real comprehension of the full impact of what he was saying. His lack of legalism enabled him to ignore the fact that, even though "tongues of *fire*" had appeared on the believers, basically there was none of what Joel prophesied manifesting in the upper room. But Peter's innate ability to tap into the Spirit's voice enabled him to travel through time and declare that "**this** *is* **that!**"

The point is that the Holy Spirit manifests Himself in ways that are *beyond* our ability to prophesy. In this case, Joel was right *and* Peter was right. But most importantly, the Holy Spirit was right! The Spirit of God is *always* right, but His ways are higher than ours. We can declare what we believe that He will do, being confident that He will honor our faith, but we must remember that everything He does is unprecedented and somewhat unpredictable, because what He does is *this* – it hasn't been done before – and He does what He does *now,* so we can never be fully prepared for it. When Jesus told Nicodemus that *"the wind blows where it wishes" (John 3:8),* He was giving us all a revelation of how the Spirit operates. The amazing thing about *this* is that it is both profound and practical at the same time. The miraculous is all around us, like the air that we breathe. We are not always awed by it, but we can never take it for granted.

What Do You Have in Your Hand?

When God assigned Moses the impossible task of bringing about Israel's exodus from Egypt, He only equipped him with *this.* In Exodus 4, Moses asked God, *"What if they don't believe me, or refuse to listen to me?"* God responded to Moses' question simply by asking another one. He asked, *"What do you **have in your hand?"** And Moses said, *"A rod."* There was nothing special or unusual about that rod. He had *already* been using it to guard and guide his father-in-law's sheep. He already owned it and was using it in his everyday life. But when Moses obeyed God, the rod became something quite different – something with amazing, miraculous properties. His *this* became a *that* through obedience. When he cast the rod on the ground, it became a living reptile, and when he picked it back up, it returned to its inanimate state. Then, when Pharaoh's magicians turned *their* rods into serpents, Moses' animal ate up the other ones.

Eventually, Moses used that very same rod to perform the most impressive wonder of his life. He stretched the rod over the Red Sea and the water parted into two halves, allowing the Israelites to cross over on dry ground. But the most remarkable part of the story about Moses' rod was that God made him use something that he *already had* in his hand. When Jesus told His disciples to announce that the Kingdom of God was "at hand," He was telling us all that the Kingdom is, in a sense, just like Moses' rod. The Kingdom is *this*. The Kingdom is *handy*. It's as close to you as is your hand. It already exists in that to which you daily put your hand! The Kingdom is revealed in everyday life. It is revealed in what is already familiar to you – in your routine, experience and personal sphere of influence. The reason it must be sought *first* (Matthew 6:33) is that it is so readily accessible that it is very easy to overlook and miss.

The gospels are full of examples of this Kingdom philosophy demonstrated through the miracles of Jesus. He always created something out of something *else* – out of *this*. He could have just *created* wine at the marriage of Cana, but instead, He turned water (*this*) into wine (*that*). He could have *created* food to feed the five thousand, but, instead, He chose to turn a boy's little lunch of five loaves of bread and two fish into enough food to accommodate the multitudes. Over and over you see Him taking the mundane and ordinary things of normal life – the things that are "at hand" – and turning them into revelations of His supernatural Kingdom on the earth. To be powerful in the Kingdom of God, you must recognize what you already have in your hand. That's where you will find your Kingdom authority. It's *already* in your world and in your consciousness. It's in what you *already* know and have. It's in *this!*

No Day But Today

This is why it is so important for you to embrace the now. The *now* is very connected to *this*. If you don't live in the *now*, you will be unable to appreciate *this*. The Tony award-winning, smash musical *RENT,* which is loosely based on Puccini's opera *La Boheme,* paints a bleak, somewhat depressing view of the lives of young, urban "bohemians" living (and dying) with HIV/AIDS in New York City. In the story, a group of HIV-positive kids meet regularly in a support group where they continually affirm that there is *"no day but today."* The whole concept of kids who "rent" rather than own is symbolic of a larger picture of transient lives cut short and is reflective of the unfortunate reality of far too many of today's youth. In the context of the play, the phrase *"no day but today"* is at once hauntingly heartbreaking and positively proactive. But, the musical is what it is and has its own realistic and modern point of view.

Even though I have seen it twice, it is not one of my favorites. I prefer art that inspires me to feel more hopeful and optimistic about life and the future. But there are two songs from the show that I really do love, because they actually convey a certain sense of a hopeful outlook in the midst of a significant life-tragedy. One is called *Seasons of Love,* which is about how to properly measure the lifespan of a person. The other is the *Finale B.* I want to share the lyrics of that one here with you. I am taking them out of their original context for my purposes, the main one being that I want you to grasp how wonderful and important your ***this*** is! You don't have to contract a life-threatening disease to make you begin to appreciate the here and now, or to realize that THIS is the day the Lord has made, or to start making the most of the time you have here. You *should* live your life as if there is *no day but today* just because ***it's all good!***

Finale B

There is no future/ There is no past
Thank God this moment's not the last!

There's only us/ There's only this
Forget regret/ Or life is yours to miss -
No other road/ No other way -
No day but today!

There's only now/ There's only here
Give in to love/ Or live in fear -
No other path/ No other way
No day but today!

– from *RENT*
Book, Music and Lyrics by Jonathon Larson

Meditations for Chapter Eight

1.

So the Lord said to him, "What is that IN YOUR HAND?" He said, "A rod." (Exodus 4:2)

2.

And it shall come to pass afterward that I will pour out My Spirit upon all flesh; your sons and daughters shall prophesy, your old men shall dream dreams, your young men shall see visions. And I will show wonders in the heavens and in the earth: blood and fire and pillars of smoke. The sun shall be turned into darkness, and the moon into blood, before the great and awesome day of the Lord. (Joel 2:28, 30, 31)

3.

And as you go, preach, saying, 'The kingdom of heaven is AT HAND." (Matthew 10:7)

4.

And He took bread, gave thanks and broke it, and gave it to them, saying, "THIS is My body which is given for you; do THIS in remembrance of Me." (Luke 22:19)

5.

But Peter, standing up with the eleven, lifted up his voice, and said unto them, Ye men of Judea, and all ye that dwell at Jerusalem, be this known unto you, and hearken to my words: For these are not drunken, as ye suppose, seeing it is but the third hour of the day. But THIS IS THAT which was spoken by the prophet Joel. (Acts 2:14-16 KJV)

6.

For I received from the Lord that which I also delivered
to you: that the Lord Jesus on the same night in which
He was betrayed took bread; and when He had given
thanks, He broke it and said, "Take, eat; THIS is My
body which is broken for you; do THIS in remembrance
of Me." In the same manner He also took the cup
after supper, saying, "THIS cup is the new covenant
in My blood. THIS do, as often as you drink it, in
remembrance of Me." (1 Corinthians 11:23-25)

7.

But without faith it is impossible to please Him, for he
who comes to God must believe that HE IS, and that
He is a rewarder of those who diligently seek Him.
(Hebrews 11:6)

Chapter Nine

One Day at a Time

And we have known that to those loving God all things do work together for good, to those who are called according to purpose.
Romans 8:28 – Young's Literal Translation

Don't judge each day by the harvest you reap, but by the seeds you plant.
— Robert Louis Stevenson

God's Kingdom is here now. In my book, *Keepin' It Real,* I went into great detail showing how the "Kingdom of God" and the "Kingdom of Heaven" are the same thing in the gospels. And because some have asked, yes, I do believe that there is a literal heaven where our recreated spirits go when our bodies die (I personally believe that it is *here* in another dimension, but I'll save that for another book). The point I want to make *here* is that the definition of the Kingdom of God/Kingdom of Heaven is simply the authority of Christ on this earth. It is wherever Jesus, the Christ (the Head of the Body) reigns through "His Christ" on this planet. It comes when the kingdoms of this world become the kingdoms of our God and of His Christ in demonstration and power. God's Kingdom in Christ manifests when His will is done on earth as it is in heaven, and Jesus gave the Church the keys with which to lock or unlock it.

I love the way Matthew 6:34 is stated in *The Message*: *"Give your entire attention to what God is doing right now, and don't get worked up about what may or may not happen tomorrow. God will help you deal with whatever hard things come up when the time comes."* The whole chapter is, of course, Jesus' masterpiece revelation of the Kingdom of God, and the best part, in my opinion, is that He ends the discourse talking about the importance of understanding that the Kingdom is in the NOW. Seeking first His Kingdom is living in the *now*, and that means living one day at a time. Even though the theme of this book is about living your *whole* past, present and future life, it is imperative that you always remember that each day is, in a sense, your whole life in microcosm. Give your entire attention to the Kingdom of God by giving your entire attention to what God is doing in your life right now – today!

It's pointless to waste today by worrying about what is coming up tomorrow, because the things that you may be dreading right now may not even happen, and the unknown is virtually impossible to prepare for anyway. Regardless of what tomorrow brings, you must face it with confidence, being totally assured that God will always perfect that which concerns you. You'll know what to do when the time comes. Jesus even told His disciples not to worry about how to defend themselves in court, because He promised that He would personally give them the appropriate words to say, if and when that time arrived. Part of living in the now is *expecting* the best, but being *prepared* for the worst. And yet, the only way to *really* be prepared for the possible worst is to plan to live in the now when the worst happens. So, whatever happens tomorrow, you'll just have to wait, in faith, and cross each bridge when you get to it.

The acronym that spells out the word *fear* is: **F**alse **E**vidence **A**ppearing **R**eal, and living in the now not only helps you to seek first the Kingdom, but it also prevents you from submitting to the threats posed by future false evidence. The real Kingdom life is a *daily* life and a *fear-free* life. Living life one day at a time allows you to keep your strength built up, so that you can run toward every giant that attempts to intimidate you, as David ran toward Goliath. You can *daily* overcome any trace of cowardice in your life and can progressively become aggressive enough to intimidate the very thing that is trying to intimidate you! Worry is depleting, and ultimately debilitating, because it keeps you spread too thin emotionally. When you channel all your energy into making each day the best that it can be, you are able to remain energized and strong, and this kind of strength keeps your vision for the future accurate and precise.

What a Difference a Day Makes

> How wonderful it is that nobody need wait a single moment before beginning to change the world.
> – Anne Frank

Abraham Lincoln said, "The best thing about the future is that it comes only one day at a time." The future is definitely coming, whether you want it to or not. But because it is coming in 24-hour increments, you don't have to be overwhelmed by it. You live in a wonderful world that your heavenly Father has created for you to enjoy, so be thankful for what He continues to bring to you on a daily basis to make your stay here a pleasurable one. Count your blessings. You were blessed as you came into this day, and you will be blessed as you go out of this day. Regardless of what has happened, and regardless of what is happening now, you have everything to look forward to in the future because the God Who works all things together for your good does so on a continuum, so that your latter is always greater than your former. Going from glory to glory is sometimes a painful experience, but it is well worth it.

Make the most of the possibilities presented to you during these 24 hours. You can't change the world in that amount of time, but you can certainly make it a little bit better than it was yesterday by improving your immediate environment today. Do everything in your power to live your life to the fullest *right now*, because maximizing your *day* is a big part of the maximum enjoyment of your *life*. If you are working today, don't just *endure* your work, *enjoy* it! Be thankful for the opportunities that your vocation affords you. Take pride in the work of your hands. Find your fulfillment in knowing that you are making a contribution to your world. Celebrate what the day represents, enjoying the journey even if you don't fully know how to locate its destination. Something could happen today that could change your life forever, so be sure to put some thought into how you are presently progressing on your path of purpose!

Open your spiritual eyes and begin to really pay attention to the needs of those around you. You are the answer to somebody's prayer, so look for windows of opportunity and then be there for that person. Look in the places where you would normally *least* expect to find a need to fill. Making a difference for someone else may be just the thing that you need to help you get your concentration off of your own problems. You cannot lead a balanced life of peace and harmony if you are always fixated on your own negatives. And remember, every little bit helps. You can't do *everything*, but you can do *something*. And, who knows? Solving a problem for someone else might even open an unseen door of promotion for you, taking you to a higher level of success. Being in the *right* place at the *right* time to do the *right* thing for the *right* person might turn what's wrong in your life *right now* toward the *right* direction!

Little Things Mean a Lot

> Sometimes when I consider what tremendous consequences come from little things – I am tempted to think there are no little things.
> – Bruce Barton

Miracles happen every day, and an awesome one – even one you've waited a lifetime for – may be just around the next corner. But remember that big things often come in small packages, so you have to be sure that you don't accidentally overlook your miracle while busily rounding that corner. The Bible is full of stories of everyday people like you and me who received huge miracles and performed enormously powerful feats and exploits, simply by being obedient in the small things. Dipping seven times in the Jordan River, making a cake for a prophet during a time of famine, or simply casting your fishing net on the other side of the boat may seem too trivial – even too silly – to even make a ripple in the grand scheme of things. But sometimes you have to be willing to do the *ridiculous* so that God can do the *miraculous,* and the very "smallness" of a thing may be what causes it to look *too* ridiculous to you.

Instead of fearing the unknown, do what you can today to make your life count positively. Seeds are little things that produce big results, and there are seeds that you can plant today that really will make a difference tomorrow. Little random acts of kindness, good words spoken to others, small preparations, specific prayer, having a good attitude – these things may seem insignificant to the big picture right now, but they certainly are not. Replace your dread with anticipation for the adventure that is coming, but enjoy the groundwork that you are doing today. You've heard it said "It's hard by the yard, but it's a cinch by the inch," and that statement, corny as it may sound, is absolutely true. Make this lyric from the Broadway musical, *Godspell,* your sincere prayer: "Day by day, day by day, O, dear Lord, three things I pray . . . to see Thee more clearly, love Thee more dearly, follow Thee more nearly, day by day . . . ."

That really sums it all up, doesn't it? Your whole world is made up of lots of little things that happen on a daily basis, so it is of the utmost importance that you pay attention to the details and that you focus on finding the day's potential. Pray that you see things more clearly *today.* Perspective can change everything, so nurture your vision, concentrating on the half of your glass that is *full.* Pray that you are able to love Him more dearly *today.* He will give you, this day, that daily bread that will keep your heart bent in His direction, because He works all things together for good for those who *love* Him! And pray that you can follow Him more nearly *today*. It's too much to ask of yourself that you try to be a Christian disciple for the rest of your life. The standard is just too high for that kind of pressure. Just pray that you can do it *today*, without making unrealistic promises for tomorrow. Day by day, ***it's all good!***

Meditations for Chapter Nine

1.
This is the DAY the Lord has made; we will rejoice and be glad in it. (Psalm 118:24)

2.
For who has despised the DAY OF SMALL THINGS? (Zechariah 4:10)

3.
Give us this DAY our daily bread.   (Matthew 6:11)

4.
Jesus said, "No procrastination. No backward looks. You can't put God's kingdom off till tomorrow. Seize the DAY." (Luke 9:62 The Message)

5.
He who would love life and see good DAYS, let him refrain his tongue from evil, and his lips from speaking deceit. (1 Peter 3:10)

6.
And so we have the prophetic word confirmed, which you do well to heed as a light that shines in a dark place, until the DAY dawns and the morning star rises in your hearts. (2 Peter 1:19)

7.

*But, beloved, do not forget this one thing, that with the
Lord one DAY is as a thousand years, and a thousand
years as one DAY. (2 Peter 3:8)*

Chapter Ten

The Awesome Power of Forgiveness

Now we know that for those who love God all things are working together for good – for those, I mean, whom with deliberate purpose He has called.
Romans 8:28 – Weymouth New Testament

> Things do not change; we change.
> – Henry David Thoreau

Forgiveness is a gift that you give yourself. In truth, it really doesn't matter if the person who hurt you *deserves* to be forgiven for what they did (or didn't do) or not. The real point on which you should focus is that you have important things to do with your life, and you want and need to move on, so you have to cut yourself free from the emotional ties that bind you to the painful past by the awesome power available to you through real forgiveness. Your past is an important part – in fact, it is one third – of your "whole" life, but your destiny does not lie in that dimension of yourself. To find destiny, you have to stop wasting your time poking around the junkyard of your old memories, looking for treasure that you simply can never find there. There's nothing for you in the past, so stop pining for it and embrace the now so that you can face the future and win at the game of life with the hand that you have been dealt.

Throughout my years of counseling (with more people than I even care to try to estimate in number), I have become convinced that on this earth there is nothing more empowering to an individual than the conscious act of forgiveness. Because it produces such profound changes in the person who sincerely practices it, it seems to him/her like it changes the whole world for the better, even though it does not. But when a person's *internal* world is changed, the *external* world immediately begins to brighten up for them and suddenly they can see their path of purpose much more clearly. In the long run, people who do not learn how to forgive never really succeed in life. It may seem that some rise to the top in spite of the pettiness and bitterness that the withholding of forgiveness creates in them, but they are not truly successful and, eventually, you will see the manifestation of their self-imposed, internal damage.

Some people actually become so addicted to the familiarity of their resentments that they don't really *want* to sever ties with the past and move on. Subconsciously, they avoid the possibilities potentially presented to them by being free of their offenses, because then they might have to take responsibility for their own level of progress in life, without the convenient luxury of blaming someone else for their inadequacies. The emotionally lazy find it much easier, and considerably more comfortable, to dwell in the past and become professional nurses of their own invisible wounds. They eventually develop the ability to recite, with perfect ease and considerable detachment, the long list of injustices done to them throughout their lives to anyone who will listen, in a continual effort to reinforce the notion that nothing has ever been *their* fault. These people prevent themselves from ever discovering the fullness of their destiny.

The bottom line is this: you can't realize destiny alone. You must have people in your life to help you become your best self, and with more people comes a greater risk of getting hurt or of being taken advantage of by someone that you need. Relationships are potential investments in the future, so they are necessary to our well-being. And that is why forgiveness is essential to the abundant life. When you forgive from the heart, you experience a sense of relief from the undeniable stress caused by the emotional demands of maintaining a grudge. Forgiveness releases you from oppression and other negative emotions, allowing you to experience a genuine flow in your life by the removal of the obstacles and barriers that you have built internally through bitterness. Many think that it is hard to forgive, but actually, it is much more difficult to maintain collective offenses, especially if you have a lot of people in your life.

Knowledge is Power

But it is important to possess a realistic grasp of the *definition* of forgiveness. You must know what it is, and what it is not, to really understand how to do it. The truth is, you can forgive without feeling obligated to condone or accept the actions of that one who may have seriously wronged you. Forgiveness is simply the release of the debt that they owe you (or that you *think* they owe you), without any expectation, realistic or not, that things will ever be the same between you again. Forgiveness is letting go of the need to be vindicated or proved to be in the right, even if you rightfully *should* expect vindication, and even if you know in your heart that you really were in the right. It is trusting that vengeance is the Lord's and that, if repayment is necessary, He is solely qualified to do it. It is realizing that, while *condoning* what "they" did is unnecessary, trying to understand *why* they did it helps the healing process.

Forgiveness is your development of effective personal time management. It is how you intentionally prevent yourself from falling into the trap of pointlessly playing internal old tapes over and over again. As many times as you spin those mental recordings of the venomous, verbal arrows shot into your innermost parts, they are just as wounding as they were when they were fresh. Then, your lack of forgiveness promotes a mutation into the practice of a kind of emotional masochism, whereby you continually inflict the same old pain on your soul. This addiction to suffering, caused by unwillingness to forgive, is unnatural and goes against the grain and flow of nature, because everything in nature – all created beings – move somehow. "Flow" is the natural course for all living things to take, and the stubborn *refusal* to forgive is a perversion that dams the flow of the human spirit and makes a mockery of the grace of God.

Forgiveness also assists in the development of effective time management for others. It allows you to stop wasting the time of those to whom you have recited your "injustice list" to the point that they can say it as well as you can, or better! Your friends may not ever tell you this, but if everyone in your world knows every disgusting detail of your tired, old war stories, it's time for you to get some new tales to tell! Besides, nothing positive ever happens by talking too much to people about other people, or about situations, over whom or which they have no control or influence. If the people to whom you confide can't do anything about the people that you need to forgive, then it is counterproductive for you, and others, to keep talking about them. Either have the courage and integrity to *go to* the person with whom you are offended and confront the issue, as Jesus taught, or admit your cowardice and just shut up about it.

> You cannot shake hands with a clenched fist.
>
> – Golda Meir

At the end of the day, the main thing that you have to face about forgiveness is determining what you *really* want out of your relationships and, ultimately, what you *really* want out of life. To do this, you have to honestly ask yourself what your priorities actually are. Put yourself to the test: Are you a peacemaker? Is proving a point more important to you than reconciliation? Can you admit when you are wrong? After someone has apologized to you, can you let it go, or do you still feel the need to punish them on some level? Does your personal universe revolve around you and your self-interests? Do you prefer to see your enemies hurt and embarrassed more than you desire to make peace with them? Is it your heart's desire to pass on the forgiveness that you have so freely received from God to others? Can you locate your attitude's source in these matters?

And the Winner is . . . LOVE!

> Many people mistake our work for our vocation. Our vocation is the love of Jesus.
> — Mother Teresa

The good news for all of us who have ever been wounded (and that's everybody) is that love – the God kind of love – never, ever fails. Jesus reigns through us as the Christ on this earth to the degree that we walk in love with one another. The keys of the Kingdom are about *remitting* the sins of others, rather than *retaining* them (John 20:23), by the power of the Holy Spirit. When love prevails, the Kingdom comes. The love of God empowers us to love the unlovable and to forgive the unforgivable, not because they deserve it or because we're so wonderful, but because Jesus Christ is Lord. Through Him, we can walk in the understanding-passing assurance that we *are* forgiven because we *have* forgiven. The greater and clearer our revelation of God's mercy for us, the more freely we are able to give mercy to others. Where their sin against us abounds, our grace for them, in Him, will *much more* abound!

As we continue to perfect the pursuit of the Christ-walk, it even becomes less overwhelming to contemplate the possibility of forgiving someone 70 x 7 times. The equation of these numbers multiplied, of course, represents *infinity*, and when Jesus introduced this concept to His disciples (Matthew 18:21, 22), they were, to say the least, probably perplexed and even astounded by it. But the more familiar and comfortable the recreated human spirit becomes with the principles of the supernatural Kingdom of God, the less abstract and unattainable 70 x 7 seems. In fact, when the Holy Spirit is allowed to testify of Jesus to your heart freely and unrestrained, the love that forgives just naturally begins to surface as the dominant life-force. 1 John 4:8 states that God *is* love. Love is His *nature* and *essence* – it is literally His DNA (if God, indeed *has* DNA!). Love is His makeup, not just an attribute that He possesses.

And because *". . . as He is, so are we in this world" (1 John 4:17)*, His obvious desire is that we <u>become</u> love, as well. Paul shared his great revelation of this fact with the Corinthians with these powerful words: *"Love never gives up. Love cares more for others than for self. Love doesn't want what it doesn't have. Love doesn't strut, doesn't have a swelled head, doesn't force itself on others, isn't always 'me first,' doesn't fly off the handle, doesn't keep score of the sins of others, doesn't revel when others grovel, takes pleasure in the flowering of truth, puts up with anything, trusts God always, always looks for the best, never looks back, but keeps going to the end. Love never dies . . . ." (1 Corinthians 13:4-8 The Message)*. When love is the dominant force in your life, forgiveness is easy to demonstrate. Love is the more excellent way and, when you live out your whole life guided by love, you can live the life that is *all good!*

Meditations for Chapter Ten

1.
Moreover if your brother sins against you, go and tell him his fault between you and him alone. If he hears you, you have gained your brother. (Matthew 18:15)

2.
Then Peter came to Him and said, "Lord, how often shall my brother sin against me, and I forgive him? Up to seven times?" Jesus said to him, "I do not say to you, up to seven times, but up to seventy times seven." (Matthew 18:21, 22)

3.
And his master was angry, and delivered him to the torturers until he should pay all that was due to him. So my heavenly Father also will so to you if each of you, from his heart, does not forgive his brother his trespasses. (Matthew 18:34, 35)

4.

Love never fails . . . (1 Corinthians 13:8)

5.

*Beloved, let us love one another, for love is of God; and
everyone who loves is born of God and knows God.
(1 John 4:7)*

6.

*Love has been perfected among us in this: that we may
have boldness in the day of judgment; because as He
is, so are we in this world. There is no fear in love; but
perfect love casts out fear, because fear involves torment.
But he who fears has not been made
perfect in love. (1 John 4:17, 18)*

7.

*If someone says, "I love God," and hates his brother, he is
a liar; for he who does not love his brother whom he has
seen, how can he love God whom he has not seen? And
this commandment we have from Him: that he who loves
God* must *love his brother also. (1 John 4:20, 21)*

Chapter Eleven

The Path to Wholeness: Harmonizing Spirit, Soul and Body

Y sabemos que a los que aman a Dios, todas las cosas les ayudan a bien, esto es, a los que conforme a su propósito son llamados.

Romans 8:28 – Spanish Bible

> We do not grow absolutely, chronologically. We grow sometimes in one dimension, and not in another; unevenly. We grow partially. We are relative. We are mature in one realm, childish in another. The past, present and future mingle and pull us backward, forward, or fix us in the present. We are made up of layers, cells, constellations.
>
> – Anais Nin

My prayer is that, by now, having reached this point in the reading, you are starting to hear a *word of reconciliation* concerning your life. I want your past, present and future selves to be *reconciled* into one whole person – a complete being who walks in the confidence that comes from believing that all things are working together for your good. A major part of understanding that word of reconciliation is tuning your life to a certain harmony of spirit, soul and body. We have established that you *are* a spirit, you *have* a soul, and you *live* in a body, but there is an even higher level of being which comes from bringing all three dimensions into oneness. To be "re-conciled" means "to become conciliatory again." Conciliation comes from the same root as does *council* and/or *counsel*, so, in this context, it means the re-formation of a *council* consisting of *past you, present you, future you, spiritual you, soulish you,* and *physical you.*

This "council" must receive "counsel" from *the Counselor* and *Prince of Peace,* Jesus Christ, because, as the Christ, He is the ultimate example of reconciliation. Jesus of Nazareth, manifested as the Christ, was and is fully integrated as a complete being and entity – the consummate revelation of the *I AM.* Jesus, as the Son of Man, walked in absolute wholeness. He was centered and focused in a way that proved He was as connected to the spirit world as He was to the natural world, and vice versa. As the Son of God, He entered the physical realm and conquered it, triumphing over death (the disconnection of the spirit from the body), and secured, once and for all, His place of total supremacy and preeminence in all things. Jesus walked in the unbroken unity of His past, present and future, as well as the perfect oneness of His spirit, soul and body. Nothing about Him was out of harmony or out of sync.

The harmonizing of these three dimensions is the way to reveal Christ in your *self* as the "hope of glory" (Colossians 1:27). After the fall, man became disconnected from *himself,* as a direct result of his disconnection from *God* through disobedience. The revelation of Christ *in* you reconciles you to God, of course, but it also provides a way to reconcile you to *yourself.* When you make Jesus your Lord, your spirit (the "pneuma") regains the ascendancy and is once again qualified to claim the leadership role over your soul (the "psyche") so that the *real you*, through your mind, will and emotions, can dominate the physical body (the "soma"). The "pneuma" (Greek for *spirit* or *breath*) now reigns as **king**. The "psyche" (Greek for *mind*, which is the major part of your *soul*) assumes the position of **servant**. And the "soma" (Greek for both *body* and **slave**) compliantly carries out the orders passed down to it from the spirit.

Jesus came to save "*that*" which was lost, so the path to wholeness is the reassignment of these lost positions. Fallen man became primarily and predominantly *physical* – an inversion of his original design, which was meant to be spiritual *first*, physical *last*. Even though God created Adam's body *before* He breathed His spirit into him, Adam's spirit already existed in God. When your Christ-ruled spirit *reigns* again, Jesus is glorified, fulfilling the "hope" of glory. The hope is the restoration of the glory lost in the fall to all who came out of Adam. As you follow the history of the return of God's departed glory, you see it first appearing, temporarily, in the tabernacle or on the mountain, as *fire* or as a *cloud* or as the *shekinah*. Later, Isaiah prophesies that the whole earth would be *filled* with it, and even goes on to say that the glory could rise *upon* you. But the ultimate "hope" is that it will not just be *around* you or *upon* you . . .

It's All Inside

> What lies behind us and what lies before us are small matters compared to what lies within us.
> — Ralph Waldo Emerson

The fulfillment is the glory coming to abide *within* the spirit of the recreated man/woman/boy/girl. This glory was and is manifested in the person of the Holy Spirit. Jesus said: *"If you love me, obey my commandments. And I will ask the Father, and He will give you another Counselor, who will never leave you. He is the Holy Spirit, who leads into all truth. The world at large cannot receive Him, because it isn't looking for Him and doesn't recognize Him. But you do, because He lives WITH you now and later will be IN you" (John 14:15-17 NLT).* God had been gradually moving toward man throughout history, revealing Himself in temples and through laws, types and shadows, until the Word could become flesh and could reconcile man to Him. Then, the new wine of the Spirit could be poured into new wineskins, who would *individually* become the living stones used to build His permanent earthly habitation.

The conventional wisdom is that each of these individuals is made up simply of body and soul, but the Scriptures speak, instead, of the "inner man" which is comprised of the eternal spirit and the eternal soul, and this eternal, inner man is housed in a temporal body which will be recreated in the resurrection. One school of thought follows that the *spirit* is changed instantly at the *new birth*, the *body* is changed instantly at the *second coming of Christ*, but the *soul* is being saved (changed), *progressively* and *gradually*, through an arduous process of mind renewal, and this "theo-logic" is quite true on one level. But, even though Hebrews 4:12 states that the sword of the living Word "divides" the soul and spirit, it is difficult to be too precise in defining the distinction between these two components of the inner man. Spirit and soul occasionally *need* to be divided in order to remove emotional impurities from true heart-faith.

Jesus said that the rebirth of the *spirit* brings about change in an individual (John 3:3-7), but Paul said that transformation comes by the renewing of the *mind* (Romans 12:1, 2). My *own* belief is that the ultimate dimension to which we should all aspire is the harmonizing, blending, melding, uniting – making the "*three* become *one*" – of spirit, soul and body. Many find this concept controversial, but I think that this is the way that we are to defeat the last enemy *("Then comes the end, when He delivers the kingdom to God the Father, when He puts an end to all rule and all authority and power. For He must reign till He has put all enemies under His feet. The last enemy that will be destroyed is death." 1 Corinthians 15:24-26),* and that Jesus is held in heaven until this is fully restored *("For He must remain in heaven until the time for the final restoration of all things . . ." Acts 3:21 NLT).*

Wholly Holy, Wholly

May God Himself, the God who makes everything HOLY and WHOLE, make you HOLY and WHOLE, put you together – spirit, soul, and body . . .
                              1 Thessalonians 5:23 The Message

In the closing words of Paul's first letter to the Thessalonians, he offers a prayer for the whole spirit, the whole soul, and the whole body: *". . . and I pray God your whole spirit and soul, and body be preserved blameless . . ."* (1 Thessalonians 5:23 KJV). In talking about making peace with the past, we have covered a lot of territory about inner healing, but the one thing that is better than being *healed* is being *made whole.* The truest definition of *"holiness"* is *"wholeness: completeness; living without deficiency."* God's best is that your spirit be made whole, as well as your body and soul. *"I pray that God, who gives peace, will make you completely holy. And may your spirit, soul, and body be kept healthy and faultless until our Lord Jesus Christ returns"* (1 Thessalonians 5:23 CEV). Because this is a prayer that is virtually *never* prayed, I want to offer a *whole* prayer for your own *wholeness . . .* agree with me as I pray the Scriptures:

> **In Jesus' name, I say that your spirit is made *whole.*** Your spirit is the candle of the Lord, searching the innermost parts of the belly, or the hidden rooms of the heart. Your strong spirit will sustain you during times of infirmity and adversity. God is revealing the things of *His* Spirit to *your* spirit, so that you, as a spiritual person, are able to judge all things *(". . . Spirit can be known only by spirit – God's Spirit and our spirits in open communion. Spiritually alive, we have access to everything God's Spirit is doing, and can't be judged by unspiritual critics" – 1 Corinthians 2:14, 15 The Message).* The blood of Jesus Christ has cleansed your spirit from all sin and has declared you righteous – in right standing with God *(". . . to the spirits of just men made perfect, to Jesus the Mediator of the*

new covenant, and to the blood of sprinkling that speaks
better things than that of Abel" – Hebrews 12:23, 24).
The Holy Spirit has made your spirit holy!

In Jesus' name, I say that your soul is made *whole*. You
are not conformed to this world, but you are transformed
by the renewing of your mind, that you may prove what
is that good, and acceptable, and perfect will of God.
You have the mind of Christ, and Jesus is made unto you
wisdom. You prosper and are in health, even as your
soul prospers. I pray for the healing of your memories,
so that you can forget those things which are behind, and
press on to what lies ahead. I pray for miraculous growth
in areas where there has been arrested development in
your soul, so that you are able to put away childish things
and become wholly mature in your thinking. I pray for the
liberation of your mind, the strengthening of your will, and
the healing of your emotions. The Lord is your shepherd
– you shall not lack wholeness. He makes you lie down in
green pastures and leads you beside the still waters. *He*
restores your soul!

In Jesus' name, I say that your body is made *whole*. The
same Spirit that raised Christ from the dead dwells in you
and quickens your mortal body. Your health springs forth
speedily. Jehovah Rapha takes sickness away from your
midst, and none of the plagues of the Egyptians come on
you because you are Abraham's seed. Jesus was wounded
for your transgressions, bruised for your iniquities; the
chastisement of your peace was upon Him, and by His
stripes you are healed. I call you free from dis-ease, and
say that the prosperity of your soul makes you physically
healthy. And I pray that as the Father, Son and Holy Ghost
are One, *you* - spirit, soul and body - become one! And,
as God said, "*the people are one, and nothing that they*
imagine to do will be impossible to them," I decree that you
are *one*, and that nothing *you* imagine will be impossible
to *you*! And I release all of my faith toward the working

of all things in all dimensions of your life to work together for your good! I speak the word of reconciliation to all the parts of you and prophesy that *it's all good!*

Meditations for Chapter Eleven

1.
He restores my SOUL . . . . (Psalm 23:3)

2.
But God has revealed them to us through His Spirit. For the Spirit searches all things, yes, the deep things of God. For what man knows the things of a man except the SPIRIT of the man which is in him?
(1 Corinthians 2:10, 11)

3.
It is sown a natural BODY, it is raised a spiritual BODY. If there is a natural BODY, there is also a spiritual BODY. So also it is written, "The first man, Adam, became a living SOUL." The last Adam became a life-giving SPIRIT. (1 Corinthians 15:44, 45 NAS)

4.
And may the God of peace Himself sanctify you through and through [separate you from profane things, make you pure and wholly consecrated to God]; and may your SPIRIT and SOUL and BODY be preserved sound and complete [and found] blameless at the coming of our Lord Jesus Christ (the Messiah).
(1 Thessalonians 5:23 AMP)

5.

*May God Himself, the God who makes everything holy
and whole, make you holy and whole, put you together
– SPIRIT, SOUL, and BODY – and keep you fit for the
coming of our Master, Jesus Christ. The One who called
you is completely dependable. If He said it, He'll do it!
(1 Thessalonians 5:23, 24 The Message)*

6

*For the word of God is living and powerful, and sharper
than any two-edged sword, piercing even to the division
of SOUL and SPIRIT, and of joints and marrow, and
is a discerner of the thoughts and intents of the heart.
(Hebrews 4:12)*

7.

*Beloved, I pray that in all respects you may prosper and
be in good health, just as your soul prospers.
(3 John 2 NASB)*

Chapter Twelve

Get Over It!

Furthermore, we know that God causes everything to work together for the good of those who love God and are called in accordance with His purpose.
Romans 8:28 – The Complete Jewish Bible

> Drop the last year into the silent limbo of the past. Let it go, for it was imperfect, and thank God that it can go.
>
> – Brooks Atkinson

It has been said that nothing is a waste of time if you use the experience wisely. A major part of perceiving purpose in your present is knowing how to properly assess the things that have happened to you throughout your life and what to do with each experience, emotionally. Was the experience positive? If so, then thank God for His goodness in bringing that thing to you, recognize it as a blessing, and draw strength from it. Were you supposed to learn a lesson from the experience? Then walk in the light of the knowledge that you have gained and pass on the information to others who might benefit from your wisdom. Was the experience a mistake? If that's the case, then learn from the mistake and be vigilant, so as not to repeat it. Was the experience just absolutely horrible and negative? Then take what you can from it, put it behind you, and move on. Find refuge in the shelter of a life lived in the *now*.

Of course, I realize that Ecclesiastes, chapter three, states that *"to every thing there is a season"* and that there is *"a time to heal."* And I am fully aware that everyone does not require the *same* time to heal from hurtful experiences. Healing takes much longer for some than it does for others. I also know that there are some things that happen in life that can affect a person so profoundly – like enduring severe abuse or experiencing the death of a child – that they can never *fully* get over them, nor even be expected to. I learned a long time ago that, even though I have enjoyed a very full life, there are things that other people have experienced with which I simply cannot empathize. In these cases, the best that I can do is help them to get in touch with the One who is *". . . touched with the feeling of our infirmities . . ." (Hebrews 4:15)* and to pray that they will have the comfort of the Holy Spirit and the peace that passes understanding.

That being stated, I must say that I *also* believe that there comes a time in the cases of most people when they just need to be told in no uncertain terms to **get over it!** I like the language used in the Amplified Bible's interpretation of these words from the lips of Jesus: *"And whenever you stand praying, if you have anything against anyone, forgive him and let it drop (leave it, let it go) in order that your Father Who is in heaven may also forgive you your [own] failings and shortcomings and let them drop" (Mark 11:25 AMP).* Are there things that you just need to let drop? Are there some dark areas of your life that you have talked about and received counsel for that just seem to get worse the more you talk about them? If so, then you probably need to simply decide to get over it! It can't be fixed by *counsel* or *12 steps* or *inner healing* or *therapy* or *deliverance.* It's a part of your life – deal with it! It is what it is – get over it!

No Excuses!

Did someone abuse you? *Get over it,* so that the memory of that person can stop dominating your inner world! Did you make a huge mistake for which you have paid dearly? *Get over it,* because it probably wasn't as bad as you think that it was! Has sin "ruined" your life? *Get over it,* knowing that where your sin abounds, God's grace much more abounds, and that if you confess your sins to Him, He is faithful and just to forgive you and cleanse you from all unrighteousness! Have you embarrassed yourself? *Get over it,* because people probably aren't thinking about you and your failures as much as you think they are, and so what if they are? Who are they to judge you? Are you at the lowest point of your life? *Get over it,* and start doing something positive to turn things around. Self-pity sure isn't getting you anywhere, so it's time to let it go . . . let it drop . . . move past it . . . forget about it . . . leave it alone . . . just get over it!

Two of my sons are part of a band that plays hard-driving, alternative Christian rock music. The name of the band is *Velocity* (aptly named), and their debut CD opens, loudly, with a powerful song called, *"Get Up."* My son, Judah, is the lead singer and has written most of the songs that the band does. He wrote the lyrics to all the songs on the album when he was eleven or twelve years old, and this particular song is one of my favorites that he wrote during that time. My youngest son, Jonah, is the band's very skilled and dynamic drummer, and when he and the other guys join together to tell you to "get up" through their music, you find yourself planning on doing just that! To get over something, you have to be willing to pick yourself up after a fall and get on with living the life that you were created to live. If God is for you, who can be against you? Jesus is praying for you to make it. You have no excuse to stay down!

Get Up!

Open your eyes/ Seek the bright light
And you will find/
That you can change your life/
Spread your wings and fly/ Fly above the sky
Don't let yourself fall/ Get up fly high
Get up and fly / Give it one more try
Get up and fly / Are you ready to fly?
Are you ready to fly?
Pick yourself up.

– from ***Velocity's*** debut album: ***Glass Half Full***
– Lyrics: Judah Swilley
– Music: David Disharoon

I wanted to share with you these words from the creative ministry of young people. They are a confirmation to the message of this chapter, because in the mouth of two or three witnesses every word is established. Henry Ford said, "Failure is only the opportunity to begin again more intelligently." I really believe in the truth of that statement. *Never* give up, *never* quit, and *never* stop believing in yourself! If you have fallen, brush yourself off and get back up again. Hold yourself to the highest standard and don't be too easy on yourself. You are a *champion*, and champions know how to keep getting up, no matter how *hard* they fall or how many *times* they fall. And whatever has stopped you in your tracks on the path to your destiny – get over it, already! Get a grip and get a life! Now, here's one more witness – one other thing entitled "GET UP!" It's an entry from my devotional book, *A Year In The Now!*, and *it's all good!*

January 19
GET UP!

For a righteous man may fall seven times and rise again . . .
(Proverb 24:16)

1. Today I will live in the now! I will live in the now because I have it in me to get back up again when I fall down. I am not just a survivor; I am more than a conqueror through Him who loves me! Because of the reality of the resurrection, I have the grace to **get up**, the power to prevail, and the will to win, even if I fall frequently.

2. Today I will **get up** out of my shackles of shame. An embarrassment is not the end. He has made me the head and not the tail, above only, and not beneath. I am the righteousness of God in Christ. I will arise and shine for my light has come, and the glory of the Lord has risen upon me!

3. Today I will **get up** out of my sewer of self-pity. A mistake is not mortal. If God is for me, who can be against me? He prepares a table for me in the presence of my enemies. No weapon formed against me can prosper, and every tongue that rises against me will be shown to be in the wrong!

4. Today I will **get up** out of my dungeon of discouragement. A defeat is not devastating. Forgetting those things which are behind, I press on to the prize. The same Spirit that raised Jesus from the dead lives in me. The joy of the Lord is my strength!

5. Today I will **get up** out of my morass of mediocrity. A failure is not forever. I can run and not be weary; I can walk and not faint. Greater is He Who is in me, than he who is in the world. I can do all things through Christ Who strengthens me!

6. Today I will **get up** out of my gulf of guilt. A fall is not fatal. Where sin abounds, grace does much more abound. He has not dealt with me after my sins, nor rewarded me according to my iniquity. He is faithful and just to forgive my sins and to cleanse me from all unrighteousness!

7. Today I will **get up**, even if I fall seven times (the number representing infinity), because Jesus is praying for me. I will never give up, because He never gives up on me. And every time I get back up, I become stronger than I was before I fell. Today I am restored, renewed, revived, refreshed and resurrected by His power, and today I will live in the now!

Father, help me to get back up today.
In Jesus' name, amen.

Meditations for Chapter Twelve

1.

*Many are the afflictions of the righteous, but the Lord
delivers him out of them all. (Psalm 34:19)*

2.

*The steps of a good man are ordered by the Lord, and
He delights in his way. Though he fall, he shall not be
utterly cast down; for the Lord upholds him with His
hand. (Psalm 37:23, 24)*

3.

*For a righteous man may fall seven times and RISE
AGAIN, but the wicked shall fall by calamity.
(Proverbs 24:16)*

4.

*ARISE [from the depression and prostration in which
circumstances have kept you – rise to a new life]! Shine
(be radiant with the glory of the Lord), for your light has
come, and the glory of the Lord is risen upon you!
(Isaiah 60:1 AMP)*

5.

*Do not rejoice over me, my enemy;
When I fall, I WILL ARISE; When I sit in darkness,
the Lord will be a light to me. (Micah 7:8)*

6.

*But when he came to himself, he said, ". . . I WILL
ARISE and go to my father . . ." (Luke 15:17, 18)*

7.

I will GET UP and go to my father, and I will say to him,
Father, I have sinned against heaven and in your sight.
So he GOT UP and came to his [own] father. But while
he was still a long way off, his father saw him and was
moved with pity and tenderness [for him]; and he ran
and embraced him and kissed him [fervently].
(Luke 15:18, 20 AMP)

Chapter Thirteen

From Genesis to Revelation

And we are conscious that all things are working together
for good to those who have love for God, and have been
marked out by His purpose.
Romans 8:28 – The Bible in Basic English

There are some things which cannot be learned quickly, and time, which is all we have, must be paid heavily for their acquiring. They are the very simplest things, and because it takes a man's life to know them, the little new that each man gets from life is very costly, and the only heritage he has to leave.

— Ernest Hemingway

The Bible is not a book. Even though the word "bible" comes from the Greek word *biblion,* which means *book or scroll*, it actually is a *collection* of sixty-six books and is closer in definition to the Spanish word *bibliotech,* which means *library*. Thirty-nine books of this diverse library are called the Old Testament, and twenty-seven others are called the New Testament. The collection consists of the varied writings of forty different authors, whose works span a window of time equivalent to about fifteen hundred years. Very few of the Bible's authors ever met one another, and many never read what the other writers penned during their different eras. Each author lived in a different time in history, and each one had a different approach, agenda and assignment to carry out. Some authors inadvertently contradicted what the other authors had to say on different subjects, which is why the Scriptures must be "rightly divided."

Let me say here that I love the Bible, I believe that the Scriptures are inspired, and I fully accept the Canon as an incarnation of the Logos word of God. As a bibliophile (a lover of books), I celebrate the diverse viewpoints of the authors of each volume. As one who proclaims God's word to my generation, I appreciate that there is as much agreement in the Scriptures as there is. As a student of history, I respect the words of antiquity and honor my brothers and sisters who lived and loved the holy writ down through the ages. As one who embraces the now, I feel a sense of oneness with all who have believed the Scriptures in different dimensions of time and am awed at how current and relevant the living Word continues to be in the 21st century. The Bible is a miracle, and, when interpreted through the life-giving Spirit of God and under His anointing, it becomes sharper than a two-edged sword – the very oracles of God.

The reason I make the point about the Bible being a *collection* of books, rather than a *single* book, is that the premise of fundamentalism is based in concept on the infallibility and inerrancy of "a book," and I view *that* kind of fundamentalism as intrinsically dangerous and quite contrary to the purposes of God and His Word. Atheists and other non-believers are quick to point out the contradictions in Scripture, using them as an excuse to doubt the validity of the Bible. But it is those very contradictions that make the Bible, for me at least, more beautiful, more interesting, and more humanly accessible. They also more clearly reveal the Bible as being truly supernatural, because, in the midst of all the contradictions, there is, ultimately, perfect *harmony* in both Testaments: *"The New is in the Old **contained**; the Old is in the New **explained**; the New is in the Old **concealed**; the Old is in the New **revealed**!"*— *St. Augustine.*

Living Epistles

The Bible begins, of course, with Moses' first book of the Torah, which is called *Genesis*. Genesis means origin, root, beginning, and source. The culmination and grand finale of the Bible is the last book, written by the Apostle John on the Isle of Patmos, called *the Revelation of Jesus Christ*. "Revelation" is from the Greek word *apokalupsis* (apocalypse), which means to unveil, uncover, make clear, lift up a curtain so all can see what is uncovered. It is not meant to be the apocalypse or "unveiling" of an antichrist, beast, dragon, or sun-clothed woman. It is the revelation of Jesus, the Christ! The point of the compiled books of the Bible is to confirm that the purpose of the beginning of all things is to ultimately reveal Christ! Without Genesis, Revelation is meaningless. Without Revelation, Genesis is pointless. This is the blueprint and foundation of the Bible, and this is the blueprint and foundation of your life.

> *You are our epistle written in our hearts, known and read by all men; clearly you are an epistle of Christ, ministered by us, written not with ink but by the Spirit of the living God, not on tablets of stone but on tablets of flesh, that is, of the heart.*
> **2 Corinthians 3:2, 3**

The purpose of the *genesis* of every created thing is to bring about a *revelation* of Christ in the earth. Your life had a genesis because your life, with all of its experiences, was meant to be a total revelation of Christ. The reason you are here is so that the Word can become flesh! The Bible, with all of its diversity, is full of contradictions and yet, from Genesis to Revelation, Christ is seen consistently in and through every book in some way, and finally has a complete apocalypse in the end. In the same way, you are a composite of many things and many influences. You are full of contradictions, just like David and Paul admitted that *they* were, and yet, Christ is being revealed through your past, present and future life. And, ultimately, as you continue to love Him and remain aware that you are called according to His purpose, you will have a complete Christ-apocalypse in the good outcome of your *whole* life.

It has been said that the soul rejoices to hear what it already knows. The reason you have no need that any man should teach you (1 John 2:27), is that you already know the truth, you just need to be reminded of it – to be delivered from spiritual amnesia. It doesn't need to be *imparted* to you as much it needs to be *revealed* in you. *"But when it pleased God, who separated me from my mother's womb and called me through His grace, to reveal His Son IN me . . . I did not immediately confer with flesh and blood" (Galatians 1:15, 16).* When you *". . . let that abide in you which you heard FROM THE BEGINNING . . ." (1 John 2:24),* then *genesis* takes on a whole new meaning and relevance for you. Seek to understand your genesis so that you can complete your revelation. Past, present and future, it's all about Christ, and ***it's all good!***

Meditations for Chapter Thirteen

1.
IN THE BEGINNING God created the heavens and the earth. Then God said, "Let there be light"; and there was light. (Genesis 1:1, 3)

2.
IN THE BEGINNING was the Word, and the Word was with God, and the Word was God. He was IN THE BEGINNING with God. All things were made through Him, and without Him nothing was made that was made. (John 1:1-3)

3.
That which was FROM THE BEGINNING, which we have heard, which we have seen with our eyes, which we have looked upon, and our hands have handled, concerning the Word of life – the life was manifested, and we have seen, and bear witness, and declare to you that eternal life which was with the Father and was manifested to us. (1 John 1:1, 2)

4.

Brethren, I write no new commandment to you, but an old commandment which you have had FROM THE BEGINNING. The old commandment is the word which you heard FROM THE BEGINNING.
(1 John 2:7)

5.

Therefore let that abide in you which you heard FROM THE BEGINNING. If what you heard FROM THE BEGINNING abides in you, you also will abide in the Son and in the Father. (1 John 2:24)

6.

Beloved, now we are the children of God; and it has not yet been revealed what we shall be, but we know that when He is revealed, we shall be like Him, for we shall see Him as He is. (1 John 3:2)

7.

The Revelation of Jesus Christ, which God gave Him to show His servants – things which must shortly take place. And He sent and signified it by His angel to His servant John. (The Revelation 1:1)

Chapter Fourteen

Now Faith Is

Moreover we know that to those who love God, who are called according to His plan, everything that happens fits into a pattern for good.

Romans 8:28 – Phillips

> If you want to build a ship, don't drum up the men to gather wood, divide the work, and give orders. Instead, teach them to yearn for the vast and endless sea.
>   – Antoine de Saint Exupery

When you change the way you look at things, the things that you look at change. That's why there are so many Scriptures that speak about *both* faith and sight, simultaneously. *Faith is the evidence of things not seen . . . we walk by faith and not by sight . . . we do not look at the things which are seen, but at the things which are not seen . . . .* Faith sees things as they are in the now, while believing that there is yet another present reality that allows us to call those things which are not as though they are. Understanding the now-ness of God releases the God-kind of faith. Faith has a voice that speaks in the present tense. It demands that you live your *whole* life according to what you *believe*, rather than by the *appearance* of the current circumstances of that life. Faith sees a bigger picture. It exposes the reality of things existent in the spirit-realm, making the sense-ruled realm much less relevant. It holds everything together.

Faith simply is not moved by what it sees. It operates by a sixth sense that receives and channels information through a different gate than the eye or the ear or the nose or the tongue or the skin. It perceives the invisible. It creates worlds and moves mountains by the exercise of dominion in the spirit-world. It changes the seen things by reshaping the unseen. It makes the material seem rather immaterial and causes matter not to matter so much. Faith is the triumph of the *spiritual* over the *physical*. It is the exaltation of the *invisible* over the *visible,* the *supernatural* over the *natural,* and the *possible* over the *impossible*. Faith destroys doubt and unbelief and rewards the renewed mind of the spirit-man by defeating the un-renewed mind of the flesh-man. Faith is spiritually logical, yet foolish and unacceptable to the human intellect. Faith is God-breathed and heaven-inspired. It always rises to the top, and it always wins.

Ralph Waldo Emerson said, "All that I have seen teaches me to trust the Creator for all I have not seen." Faith sees everything through eyes of trust – trust that does not lean unto its own understanding. I read somewhere that faith is believing in *advance* what can only be understood in *reverse*. The reason it is so important to grasp these concepts is this: all things *do* work together for your good if you love God and are called according to His purpose, but you have to *believe* that those things are working together for good to make it happen. The "good" does not just automatically find you. You must apply the pressure of your faith to the circumstances of your life to make them line up with the Word of God concerning your destiny. Your positive attitude and words of faith will actually *attract* the good to your life and will *repel* the negative forces that try to thwart the productive working together of all things.

Make it Happen!

> If I were dying, my last words would be, have
> faith and pursue the unknown end.
> — Oliver Wendell Holmes, Jr.

You create the world in which you live by your faith-filled words. God created *His* worlds by the words of His mouth, and you create *your* own environment or "world" in the same way. You are today a product of what you said yesterday. Tomorrow you will have and be what you are saying today. God maintains *His* worlds by the words of *His* mouth, and you maintain the quality of *your* world by the creative and authoritative words of *your* mouth. Your words can be productive or destructive, life-giving or death-inducing, because you are in the God-class – a partaker of the divine nature. You must have faith in your faith by believing your beliefs and doubting your doubts, because the life of faith is the only life that pleases God. "Pursuing the unknown end" is the way to retain a reservation for a seat in heavenly places. When you are adventurously creative through your faith, you make your Father very proud.

The great evangelist Dwight L. Moody said, "A little faith will bring your soul to heaven, but a lot of faith will bring heaven to your soul." That really is the Kingdom message in microcosm. Walking in faith is not about just trying to make it to heaven when you die. It's about taking dominion on the earth – about causing His will to be done on earth as it is in heaven, *now*. And that dominion is worked out through victoriously living the life that you were meant to live. It means taking what has been given you and making the most of all of it, even overcoming life's harshest realities by believing that they are working *for* you, rather than *against* you. God is God, and beside Him there is no other. But if you want Him to work all things together for your good, you've got to make some things happen *by faith*. But faith without work(s) is dead, so *you* have to get to work if you want *Him* to get to work in your behalf.

It's a New Day!

Take the first step in faith. You don't have to see the whole staircase, just take the first step.
– Martin Luther King, Jr.

Section One of this book dealt with pursuing peace with your *past*. When you view the past, look at it through eyes of faith and don't be moved by what you see back there. Faith is the evidence of things *not* seen, so when you remember the things that have happened along your journey, try to notice the details that you have overlooked before. This time, when you browse through your mental and emotional photo album, look for God's appearance somewhere in every picture. As you gaze at the snapshot of each memory, you will see His image prominently displayed in the foreground or center of many of them. In the good times, and in seasons of blessing, His presence is obvious. In other memory-pictures, you will have to look, deeply, to see Him standing somewhere in the shadowy background, His features difficult to make out. In these you will have to "see" by faith that it *was* Him in the picture and that He was there all along.

In Section Two, we covered material about perceiving purpose in your *present*. Right now there may be so much happening in your life – your plate may be so full – that your tendency to be overwhelmed by it all prevents you from seeing, by faith, that the hand of God is *all over* your current circumstances. Everything that is happening, presently, has His fingerprints on it, even if the evidence of those prints is invisible to the naked eye. You have to look beyond the veil to see that right now, in this very moment, even with everything that is going on *today*, for good or for bad, God really is working all things together for your good! If you sincerely submit every single situation to Him, allowing the government of it all to remain on His shoulder, you may be assured that He will continue to have everything under control. God is not worried about your life. Jesus is praying for you even as you read this. By faith, *it's all good!*

But before we move on to the third section of the book, which deals with fearlessly facing your *future*, I have a prophetic announcement to make to you, and here it is:

> By the power vested in me through the call of God on my life, and by the authority of Jesus Christ, Who presented me as a gift to His Body *(". . . He led captivity captive, and gave gifts to men . . . some to be apostles, some prophets, some evangelists, some pastors and teachers." – Ephesians 4:8, 11)*, I announce to you, in Jesus' name, that today is a new day for you! And I command the "things" of your life – the events, occurrences, happenings, and circumstances of your past and present – to get to work! I also command these things to start working together in harmony for the common goal of bringing about your ultimate good! I speak a delivering word to free you from your past, and I decree that things in the present are coming into divine order for you! Step into the now and claim ownership of this new day as you begin the next chapter of your good life. I say that your thoughts line up with God's thoughts, and that your words are in agreement with His words. Shake off every negative thought and rise up, in faith, to embrace every good thing that this new day brings to you! As you move into your future by faith, know that your steps are ordered, your destiny is unfolding, and your latter will be greater than your former! Don't be reluctant to rejoice – you have everything to look forward to. It really is a new day for you, and it starts NOW! Seize it by faith, because it's about to get really good!

Now, it's on to Section Three, and *on to the future!*

Meditations for Chapter Fourteen

1.

Behold the proud, his soul is not upright in him; But the just shall live by FAITH. (Habakkuk 2:4)

2.

For in it the righteousness of God is revealed from FAITH to FAITH; as it is written, "The just shall live by FAITH." (Romans 1:17)

3.

Therefore [inheriting] the promise is the outcome of FAITH and depends [entirely] on FAITH, in order that it might be given as an act of grace (unmerited favor), to make it stable and valid and guaranteed to all his descendents – not only to the devotees and adherents of the Law, but also to those who share the FAITH of Abraham, who is [thus] the father of us all. As it is written, I have made you the father of many nations. [He was appointed our father] in the sight of God in Whom he believed, Who gives life to the dead and speaks of the nonexistent things that [He has foretold and promised] as if they [already] existed. (Romans 4:16,17 AMP)

4.

While we do not look at the things which are seen, but at the things which are not seen. For the things which are seen are temporary, but the things which are not seen are eternal. (2 Corinthians 4:18)

5.

For we walk by FAITH, not by sight. (2 Corinthians 5:7)

6.

*NOW FAITH IS the assurance (the confirmation, the
title deed) of the things [we] hope for, being the proof of
things [we] do not see and the conviction of their reality
[faith perceiving as real fact what is not revealed to the
senses]. (Hebrews 11:1 AMP)*

7.

*But without FAITH it is impossible to please Him, for he
who comes to God must believe that He is, and that He is
a rewarder of those who diligently seek Him.
(Hebrews 11:6)*

SECTION THREE

FEARLESSLY FACING YOUR FUTURE

Fearlessly facing your future is the final step to successfully living your whole life.

·T·O·M·O·R·R·O·W·

◦T◦ is for **trust.** *Trust in the Lord with all your heart, and lean not on your own understanding; In all your ways acknowledge Him, and He shall direct your paths. (Proverbs 3:5, 6)*

. . . fearlessly face your future,
with absolute **trust** in God. He has never given you any reason
to distrust Him, or to doubt His faithfulness to you, so do not
insult His fidelity and integrity by fearing tomorrow . . .

◦O◦ is for **open.** . . . *See, I have set before you an **open** door, and no one can shut it* . . . *(Revelation 3:8)*

. . . fearlessly face the **open** door that is before you.
A whole new world lies just beyond it,
so go ahead and walk on through . . .

◦M◦ is for **move.** *For in Him we live and **move** and have our being* . . . . *(Acts 17:28)*

. . . fearlessly face your future,
and don't be reluctant to **move** when it is the right time to do so.
The wind of the Spirit blows where it wills,
so always be willing to go with the flow . . .

◦O◦ is for **overcome.** *And he who **overcomes**, and keeps My works until the end, to him I will give power over the nations. (Revelation 2:26)*

. . . fearlessly face your future,
knowing that you *can* **overcome** anything and everything,
because you were destined to rule nations . . .

◦**R**◦ is for **run.** *But they that wait upon the Lord shall renew their strength; they shall mount up with wings as eagles; they shall **run**, and not be weary. . . . (Isaiah 40:31 – KJV)*

. . . fearlessly face your future,
with no intention of slowing down. It's time to **run** into
tomorrow, without being weary, because you haven't even gotten
to the best part of your life yet . . .

◦**R**◦ is for **run.** *. . . Write the vision and make it plain on tablets, that he may **run** who reads it. (Habakkuk 2:2)*

. . . fearlessly face your future,
and **run** toward it with the living, running vision that God has
written on the tablet of your heart . . .

◦**O**◦ is for **onward.** *Whenever the cloud was taken up from above the tabernacle, the children of Israel would go **onward** in all their journeys. (Exodus 40:36)*

. . . fearlessly face your future,
progressing **onward**, past your fears, insecurities, self-doubts
and failures, toward a whole new you that will live the life of one
who is the head and not the tail . . .

◦**W**◦ is for **wisdom.** *God alone made it possible for you to be in Christ Jesus. For our benefit God made Christ to be wisdom itself . . . . (1 Corinthians 1:30 NLT)*

. . . fearlessly face your future one day at a time,
fully confident that you will have the **wisdom** to know how to
deal with each thing as it comes . . .

I have a lot of things to

prove to myself. One is

that I can live my life

fearlessly.

- Oprah Winfrey

Chapter Fifteen

Shaping the Future by Creative Imagination

We know that God works out everything for the good of those who love Him. They are the people who are part of His plan.
Romans 8:28 – Worldwide English New Testament

> Toto, I don't think we're in Kansas, anymore.
> – Dorothy Gale

There's an old proverb that says "He who never walks except where he sees other men's tracks will make no discoveries." The only thing that you can change about your past is your perception of it, and that may actually be all that you can change about your present. But your *future* is a different story altogether! You really can do something about that, because you have the power, by your God-given creativity, to use your God-given imagination to shape tomorrow into something really wonderful. You can think outside the box. You can be original. You can boldly go where no man has ever gone before. The sky is the limit, because God does exceedingly, abundantly above all that you can ask or think *according to* the power that works within you, and that power is your creative imagination. He loves when you *ask* big, so that He can meet your needs, but He *really* loves when you *think* big, so that He can out-think you!

Creativity involves breaking out of the patterns that you have established over your lifetime and looking at future things in a different way. By the help of the Holy Spirit, you can be inventive in prayer, and prophetically experimental, as you grow in grace and even take risks in your walk of faith. Walking in the spirit often means breaking the rules, even being willing to make mistakes, knowing that, if you do, He will *still* perfect that which concerns you! By trusting Him in this way, you can remove the fear of failure from your consciousness. And liberation from the fear of failure, along with deliverance from concern over criticism, will bring you into a place of peace that really passes your understanding – a peace that ultimately enables you to rid yourself of all self-imposed limitations. The peace of God can cause you to be daring and different because, in the absence of fear, you discover all that you have within yourself.

Of course, it is important for you to guide your affairs with discretion (Psalm 112:5) and to walk in the discipline that is the result of the spiritual fruit of self-control. However, if you are too bent on being too practical, you will be too limited in your imagination to be able to shape your future in any significantly positive way. People of faith cannot allow themselves to become creatures of the commonplace or slaves to the ordinary. God did not bring you through the fire without the smell of smoke just so you could play it safe! He has been working all things together for your good to help you develop an integrity of purpose paired with an imaginative vision that will enable you to glorify Him through your exploits of faith. That sense of purpose, along with the force of that vision, will require you, at some point, to let go of all of your certainties except for the certainty that your God is a good God. Sometimes, that is all you really need to know.

> Creativity, as has been said, consists largely of rearranging what we know in order to find out what we do not know. Hence, to think creatively, we must be able to look afresh at what we normally take for granted.
>
> – George Kneller

Jesus said that if your eye is healthy, your whole body will be filled with light. Creativity *is* light. Before God created anything else He said, "Let there be light." Perception and seeing by faith

– dreams, vision, imaginative ideas – all of it – shines a light on your path. Changing the way you see what is already around you is recognizing that the Kingdom is at hand. It means turning on a light to see what you already have at your disposal – and not just so you can be grateful and appreciative. You turn on the light of creativity so that you can take your success in life to the next level. "Anyone can make the simple complicated. Creativity is making the complicated simple." – Charles Mingus

Imagine!

> I am enough of an artist to draw freely upon my imagination. Imagination is more important than knowledge. Knowledge is limited. Imagination encircles the world.
>
> – Albert Einstein

When you look up the word *imagination* in the concordance for the 1611 version of the King James Bible, you will rarely, if ever, find it mentioned in a positive light. Typically, it is used to refer to the "wicked imaginations" of men and how God dealt with them according to the evil that came from those thoughts. In other Bible translations, you usually find "imaginations" *replaced* by "thoughts," but for those conservative theologians who consider the Elizabethan English of the KJV to be the only language authorized to convey God's message, the word *imagination* remains generally taboo. As a rule, the people who look through this window of interpretation consider words like *imagination* or *visualization* to be too closely linked with New Age philosophy, or even with divination, and I understand why they see things the way they do. I don't agree with them, but I understand the way they think.

In Genesis 11:6, God says that because the people were one, nothing that they imagined to do would be impossible to them.

Of course, in this context, He was saying that they needed to be stopped from carrying out their evil plans, but in using this phrase He gave the world a revelation of the power of *unity,* as well as that of *imagination.* In many ways, what happened on the Day of Pentecost was in direct response to what happened at the Tower of Babel, with language being the main focal point concerning collective imagination. At Babel, He confounded their language to break their unity; at Pentecost, He gave them a unified language of the Spirit that enabled those who heard Peter's words to imagine an outpouring on "all flesh." That oneness, or unity of all flesh, is the main purpose of the Body of Christ. I personally believe that Jesus is "held in the heavens" until genuine unity is restored in the church on the earth.

This may be a bit of a stretch, but if you really discern the lyrics to John Lennon's song *Imagine* with an open mind, you won't hear the ranting of an atheist who doesn't believe in heaven or hell. Rather, if you listen with your heart, you will more likely discover a plea for global unity, seasoned with a disdain for the divisiveness of religion. I know that those who are deeply dispensationalist in their theology are horrified by the idea of imagining a world that is "one." The fear of a one-world government headed by an antichrist is foundational to the fear that is *essential* to fueling dispensationalist dogma. Again, I really do understand their viewpoint and, again, I really don't agree with it. I believe that there is *supposed* to be a one-world government, where every knee shall bow and every tongue shall confess to the glory of God that Jesus Christ is Lord! You may think that I'm a dreamer, but I'm not the only one! Can you *imagine!*

Get the Picture?

"Woe to those who devise iniquity, and work out [plan] evil on their beds! At morning light they practice it, because it is in the power of their hand" (Micah 2:1). In this verse, once again, you see the *concept* of imagination used in a negative light, yet it conveys the *power* of imagination, the implication being that

it gives you the ability to carry out, externally, what you have pictured, internally. Along these lines, Jesus, in His Sermon on the Mount, said that *fantasizing* about adultery was the same thing as *committing* adultery (Matthew 5:27, 28). If you read between the lines, you see a case being made for the power of imagination. In other words, if *imagining* adultery is *committing* adultery, then why couldn't you say that *imagining* success or prosperity is *having* success and prosperity? Life *and* death are in the power of the tongue, and life *and* death are in the power of the imagination. It can be used for good or evil.

The point is that faith needs imagination to become the substance of things hoped for. Jacob, by having a paradigm shift due to a divine dream, became a wonderful example of someone who understood imagination and visualization. He caused cattle to give birth to spotted and speckled calves by creating a visualization technique (spotted and speckled rods set before their watering troughs) that their bovine brains could grasp. In fashioning the coat of many colors for his son, Joseph, he gave the boy a way to imagine that all of his dreams could come true – and they did! All real people of faith are dreamers and visionaries, because it takes imagination to locate the evidence of things not seen. Creative imagination is the only way to fly somewhere over the rainbow – to shape the future by faith. Jacob used that ability to make great things happen. *You* have that same faith available to you, and that kind of faith dreams in Technicolor!

A New Way to Think

> Man's mind stretched to a new idea never goes back to its original dimensions.
> – Oliver Wendell Holmes

As we have already said, when reviewing the past or perceiving the present, you must release all of your regrets, see the big picture, and believe that what has happened or what is happening is all working together for your good. But visualizing the future requires you to draw from other mental and spiritual resources entirely. Developing a picture of the future through imagination is altogether different from simply changing your perception of the past and present. The past and present need your understanding and insight. The future needs your faith, and your faith needs your imagination! Proverbs 23:7 is frequently misquoted and taken out of context, but the truth of it remains: *"For as he thinks in his heart, so is he . . . ."* As you *think* – as you *imagine* the future – so will you be and so will your future be! Faith and imagination expand the borders of your mind, creating a greater capacity for a greater tomorrow.

At the beginning of this chapter, one of my favorite Scriptures concerning this concept was mentioned, but I like the Amplified Bible's version of Ephesians 3:20, 21 the best: *"Now to Him Who, by (in consequence of) the [action of His] power that is at work within us, is able to [carry out His purpose and] do superabundantly, far over and above all that we [dare] ask or think [infinitely beyond our highest prayers, desires, thoughts, hopes, or dreams] – To Him be glory in the church and in Christ Jesus throughout all generation forever and ever. Amen (so be it)."* I especially appreciate the word "dare," because that's really what imagination is all about. You must dare to believe that your latter will be greater than your former. You must dare to believe that your divine destiny is daily unfolding for you. You must dare to dream, creatively shaping your future life, daring to believe that *it's all good!*

Meditations for Chapter Fifteen

1.
. . . and now nothing they have IMAGINED they can do will be impossible for them. (Genesis 11:6 AMP)

2.

*Then he dreamed, and behold, a ladder was set up on
the earth, and its top reached to heaven; and there the
angels of God were ascending and descending on it.
Then Jacob awoke from his sleep and said, "Surely the
Lord is in this place, and I did not know it."
(Genesis 28:12, 16)*

3.

*Now Jacob took for himself rods of green poplar and
of the almond and chestnut trees, peeled white strips in
them, and exposed the white which was in the rods. And
the rods which he had peeled, he set before the flocks
in the gutters, in the watering troughs where the flocks
came to drink, so that they should conceive when they
came to drink. So the flocks conceived before the rods,
and the flocks brought forth streaked, speckled, and
spotted. (Genesis 30:37-39)*

4.

*Now Israel loved Joseph more than all his children,
because he was the son of his old age. Also he made him
a tunic of many colors. (Genesis 37:3)*

5.

*Your eyes are windows into your body. If you open your
eyes wide in wonder and belief, your body fills up with
light. (Matthew 6:22 The Message)*

6.

*It's what we trust in but don't yet see that keeps us going.
(2 Corinthians 5:7 The Message)*

7.

*You know that under pressure, your faith-life is forced
into the open and shows its true colors
(James 1:3 The Message)*

Chapter Sixteen

Building Vision by the Speaking Forth of Possibilities

We know that by turning everything to their good God co-operates with all those who love him, with all those that He has called according to His purpose.
Romans 8:28 – The Jerusalem Bible

> Champions aren't made in the gyms. Champions are made from something they have deep inside them – a desire, a dream, a vision.
>
> – Muhammed Ali

The quality of your future is determined by the quality of your vision for it. When you begin to explore the prospects of living your whole life long, integrating your past and present with your future, and believing that all of it is working together for your good, it is easy to draw certain conclusions about what tomorrow holds. The easiest conclusion at which to arrive is the one that assumes that whatever is to be will inevitably be, and you just have to make the best of it because, ultimately, *it's all good.* But, the truth is that your future can play out in any number of scenarios, and each of your potential "futures" awaits you in your own eternity. You must choose the future that should and will become *your* reality by building the right vision for it now. As you declare the end from the beginning, drawing on the acquired wisdom from the past and present, you can cast the deciding vote that determines which future will become yours.

If you've read this far, you obviously have a real desire to discover all of the possibilities that you can create through your life experiences to make a worthwhile difference in the world. You know that God has been speaking to you all of your life, even when you weren't trying to listen to Him. It is likely that you even heard His voice when you were a child and, although you can't see the entire *big picture* yet, you know that you're special and unique. You probably shouldn't *say* that to anyone because it would make you sound arrogant and conceited, but deep inside you know who you are and that's why you're reading this book. You already grasp these truths, you just need confirmation and reinforcement so that you can live the life that you know you should be living. The dissatisfaction that you often feel is positive, even necessary, because it keeps you stretching and reaching for something higher – something visionary.

Because you have a vision, you don't follow the crowd, which is good, because those who follow the crowd usually will get no further than the crowd. The great thing about walking your own path alone sometimes is that it makes it possible for you to find yourself in places no one has ever been! God is always interested in doing a new thing, and that's why He births vision in you by giving you the desires of your heart as you delight yourself in Him (Psalms 37:4). He actually places the desires *within,* as you intentionally conform to His will. *His* part is the *birthing* of vision. *Your* part is the *building* of vision – and your words are the building blocks of that vision, which is the substance of your future, which is the third of your whole life over which you have the most control. You can only change your *perception* of the past and present, but you can actually *create* a good part of your future.

Albert Einstein said, "There are only two ways to live your life. One is as though nothing is a miracle. The other is as though everything is a miracle." By simply accepting what the future brings as being things as they are "supposed to be," you relinquish your rights to the miraculous. But when you fill your words with faith, continuously talking up your dreams and visions, you speak forth possibilities that shape tomorrow for the good or better. Those words travel in time into the future and begin to rearrange and change the predetermined things that were starting to become inevitable in your life. If you want miracles, you can have them, but you have to *welcome* them into your own realm by the attractive words that you speak about your future. Words that build vision are like magnets for the miraculous. They outline and define the parameters of the future and are powerful little time machines that take you where you want to go.

Verbalizing Vision

Testimony:
Vision is built by testimony.

In the book of Revelation, the *word of testimony* was given equal importance to *the blood of the Lamb* for the overcoming of the accuser of the brethren. David built up his vision for destroying Goliath the giant, by rehearsing before King Saul his testimony of killing the lion and the bear. This is a classic example of how you can draw strength from the past and translate that strength into a vision for the future. Turning testimony into prophecy means that if you did *that* you can do *this*, so that, in the future, you can even do *that!* This process is one of the easiest, yet most effective, ways to integrate past, present and future. Remember what you have already accomplished and talk about it. Remember what you have already overcome and tell someone your story. And remember, *". . . He who has begun a good work in you will complete it until the day of Jesus Christ" (Philippians 1:6).*

Prophecy, Tongues and Interpretation: Vision is built by the Spirit.

Five of the nine Gifts of the Spirit, or *Charismata,* listed in
1 Corinthians 12:8-10, have to do with speech – the *word* of
wisdom, *word* of knowledge, (*word* of) prophecy, diversities of
tongues, and the interpretation of those *tongues.* Conventional
pneumatology (study of the Holy Spirit) relegates these gifts to
very precise definitions – ones that I never thought to question
throughout my Pentecostal/Charismatic history. But at this point
in my living relationship with Parakletos, the Helper, I find that I
have moved away from the confinement of those definitions and
now see the list of the Spiritual Gifts simply as proof that the
Spirit of God is very creative in His communication skills. Paul's
list, for me, now represents diversity, imagination, and a reminder
that the Paraclete can and will speak to and through me (and you),
via an infinite variety of media.

Confession of the Word: Vision is built through confession of the Word of God.

The Roman Centurion garnered Jesus' attention and effusive
praise by illustrating that he completely understood the power of
words spoken with authority. Jesus "marveled" at the confidence
that this man showed in the word of healing (*". . . speak the word
ONLY . . ." – Matthew 8:8 KVJ*), and even said to His disciples
that it was evidence of the greatest faith He had seen in all of
Israel. The single-minded person who determines to speak the
word *only* concerning his or her future, will find out, firsthand,
that the Word really does not return void. It accomplishes the
thing for which it is sent. The Centurion said to Jesus, *"For I also
am a man under authority, having soldiers under me. And I say to
this one, 'Go,' and he goes; and to another, 'Come,' and he comes
. . ." – Matthew 8:9.* If you are under authority, you can send your
words ahead of you to start preparing your future.

Calling those things that are not as though they are: Vision is built by speaking faith.

God called Abram *"Abraham"* ("father of nations") before he was the father of anything or anyone. Eventually, Abram legitimately was called Abraham by everyone, because he finally did become a father and, ultimately, a father of *many* nations. But God, in His timeless perfection, called him "father of nations" before it was appropriate to do so. Real faith is often inappropriate, and necessarily so, because faith is not bound to time. Those who *are* bound to time limitations usually find faith-talk extremely frustrating. Calling things that are not as though they are is an efficient way to travel through time, as is believing you receive when you pray (Mark 11:24). Faith is now and it positively affects tomorrow. In this context, "calling those things which are not" is the adamant refusal to allow the past or present to impose any limits on the future.

A Good Report: Vision is built by giving a good report.

In the 13th and 14th chapters of Numbers, we see that Joshua and Caleb never denied the validity of the report of the other ten spies concerning the conditions in Canaan. They never said that there weren't giants in the land, nor did they deny the fact that the cities were fortified. But their good report made a demand on another reality – one that was based on the authority of God's word, instead of by the perception of things as they appeared. Vision is built – not by denying that negative or evil things exist that could potentially affect the future, but – by giving a good report, regardless of the current circumstances. *"Finally, brethren, whatever things are true . . . noble . . . just . . . pure . . . lovely . . . of GOOD REPORT, if there is any virtue and if there is anything praiseworthy – meditate on these things" (Philippians 4:8).*

Anointed Preaching and Teaching:
Vision is built through anointed ministry.

Faith comes by *hearing* the Word, not by *having heard* it. The continuous and regular hearing of anointed preaching and teaching stimulates and activates the part of your spirit that sees into the future and the part of your soul (brain/mind) that produces vision. Deep calls unto deep. Iron sharpens iron. When the word of God is proclaimed under the unction of the Holy Spirit, it moves things in the atmosphere and sets things in motion that have been standing still, internally and externally. When your heart embraces that word, it releases your prophetic potential so that you can deliberately declare your destiny and set the future in order. The freshly-digested bread of heaven energizes and fuels your inner man, enabling you to run into the next glory and not be weary – to walk into tomorrow and not faint! When you hear the "yes," let your heart say, "amen!"

Inspired Conversation:
Vision is built by talking to others about God.

Every day of your life you are given the opportunity to speak up for the goodness of God and to elaborate on how He works all things together for you so that you can regularly experience that goodness. *"Then those who feared the Lord spoke to one another, and the Lord listened and heard them; so a book of remembrance was written before Him for those who fear the Lord and who meditate on His name" (Malachi 3:16).* This Scripture says that an actual book of remembrance is kept, containing all of your good words spoken about your good God. This is why it's so important to surround yourself with positive, faith-filled people – people who can volley the verbal ball back to your side of the conversational court. In talking with them, you are able to brainstorm about your future and develop a vision for unlimited possibilities.

Speak Up!

Just like professional boxers and wrestlers declare what is going to happen in the ring or on the mat before the fight, you must locate your inner champion and predict your own victory. They do so with great bravado to fortify their confidence, intimidate their opponent, and convince the crowd that the fight is going to be worth watching. In many ways, every day of your life is a fight and, like the professional fighters, you have to publicly – and with great audacity – call yourself a winner in every one of those days. My grandmother, Addie Mae, used to say to me, *"Son, it's a poor rooster who won't crow for his own barnyard,"* and I believed her. You've got to speak up for own your life! Talk up your own future! Your future is not in your *palm* to be read by a fortune teller; your future is in your *mouth* – you can foretell it yourself! And when you don't know specifically what to say about it, just say, **"It's all good!"**

Meditations for Chapter Sixteen

1.

Your servant has killed both lion and bear; and this uncircumcised Philistine will be like one of them, seeing he has defied the armies of the living God. Moreover David said, "The Lord, who delivered me from the paw of the lion and from the paw of the bear, He will deliver me from the hand of this Philistine." And Saul said to David, "Go, and the Lord be with you!"
(1 Samuel 17:36, 37)

2.

The centurion answered and said, Lord, I am not worthy that thou shouldest come under my roof; but speak the word only, and my servant shall be healed.
(Matthew 8:8 KJV)

3.
... God, who gives life to the dead and calls those things which do not exist as though they did ... (Romans 4:17)

4.
... God ... Who gives life to the dead and speaks of the nonexistent things that [He has foretold and promised] as if they [already] existed. (Romans 4:17 AMP)

5.
How then shall they call on Him in whom they have not believed? And how shall they believe in Him of whom they have not heard? And how shall they hear without a preacher? And how shall they preach unless they are sent? As it is written: "How beautiful are the feet of those who preach the gospel of peace, who bring glad tidings of good things!" (Romans 10:14, 15)

6.
Each person is given something to do that shows who God is: Everyone gets in on it, everyone benefits. All kinds of things are handed out by the Spirit, and to all kinds of people! The variety is wonderful:

wise counsel
clear understanding
simple trust
healing the sick
miraculous acts
proclamation
distinguishing between spirits
tongues
interpretation of tongues

All these gifts have a common origin, but are handed out one by one by the one Spirit of God. He decides who gets what, and when. (1 Corinthians 12:7-11 The Message)

7.

*And they overcame him by the blood of the Lamb and by
the word of their testimony, and they did not love their
lives to the death. (Revelation 12:11)*

Chapter Seventeen

Developing Destiny by Transcending Time

And we know that in all things God works for the good of those who love Him, who have been called according to His purpose.
Romans 8:28 –Today's New International Version

> Don't say you don't have enough time. You have exactly the same number of hours per day that were given to Helen Keller, Pasteur, Michelangelo, Mother Teresa, Leonardo da Vinci, Thomas Jefferson, and Albert Einstein.
> — H. Jackson Brown

People do what they want to do. I have spent the majority of my life working with and leading people, and have rarely, if ever, seen an exception to this rule. I've seen this principle confirmed in my own life, time and time again, as I have found amazing ways to make time to do the things that I wanted to. I have also found myself procrastinating on some other things to the point that I just convinced myself that I didn't have the time to get those things done. But the truth is that I didn't have the time because I didn't *want* to have the time. For years I said that I didn't have time to write books because of all of my responsibilities, but I have now broken through in that area to the point that I actually wrote *another* book after I started this one, and it's about *physical fitness* (*Body-Life Now!*), which is also something that I used to say I didn't have time for! *And* I wrote these two books during a major building program at CITN.

Destiny is revealed through process, and a part of that process is learning how to master your time. If you don't master time, it will master you, and the best way to master it is to transcend it, altogether, by altering the way that you perceive and interpret it. As you get older, you become increasingly aware of how fast time is always moving, and you realize that you must learn how to make the most of the time that you have. When you were a year old, one year was 100% of your life. But with every trip that you have taken around the sun on this earth-ship, a year has become relatively shorter and shorter when compared to your lifespan. As a child anticipating and looking forward to your birthday, it seemed to you like it took *forever* for that birthday to arrive. But as the birthdays kept coming throughout your life, they somehow sped up to the point that it seems to you now that they never *stop* coming, and they arrive faster and faster!

From Genesis 1:1-5 we see that the earth was created before there was the light and the darkness, which we refer to as day and night. He created light before He created the sun and the other celestial bodies that give us our natural illumination. Light comes from somewhere inside God, which is why, in his revelation, John referred to *the Lamb* as the light of the City of God. John said that the light coming from the Lamb made the sun unnecessary and obsolete. When God's ultimate purposes in creation are finally accomplished, the earth will return to its eternal state where there is no time, and Jesus, the Lamb, will be the light of the whole universe. Jesus told His disciples that He would be with them until the end of "the age," which is translated from the Greek word *"aion."* The meaning of the statement is that He promised His abiding presence with them until there is no more time. Transcending time is the will of God.

God is referred to as *The Ancient of Days* in the book of Daniel (Daniel 7:9, 10, 13, 14), which means that He is the one who existed before there were days – the one who is older than the advent of days. Throughout the Bible we see these kinds of themes of transcending time over and over again. *". . . One day with the Lord is as a thousand years, and a thousand years as one day"* (2 Peter 3:8). The prophet Joel said that God would actually *restore* years to His covenant people, and Paul commanded the Ephesians to *redeem* the time because the days were evil. God told

Moses that He was the I AM, and Jesus said the first shall be last, and the last shall be first. When He told His disciples to believe they receive when they pray (Mark 11:24), He was telling them that they could transcend time by not having to wait to believe until they saw the manifestation. All of these Scriptures, titles and concepts are about the possibility of conquering time.

Creating Time

> You will never find time for anything. If you want time, you must make it.
>
> – Charles Buxton

When I was a young man in college, I had a professor of homiletics (the art and science of preaching) that I liked very much. Besides being a busy academic, Dr. Richardson was also a full-time pastor, and he told our class about his previously having left the pastorate in order to pursue a higher degree in education. His intention in resigning his church was to have more time to study and write, but he found that with more time on his hands, he actually got less done. So he decided to resume his position as pastor, and then he was able to better manage his free time and successfully received another degree. He was living proof that, as the saying goes, if you want something done, you should ask a busy person. Time *can* be created through the power of desire and intention, and if you can create it, you certainly can *manage* it and, ultimately, *transcend* it.

The more you do, the more you *can* do. Your decision to accomplish a thing initiates your creative ability, enabling you to do more than you thought you could. The things that you make time for are the things that are most important to you, and they help reveal to you who you really are, which reveals your destiny. The decisions you make about the usage of your time change the circumstances of your life. Decisions command response, create events, and call provision. But to make important decisions, you have to stop making excuses. You have to stop saying "I don't have the time," because that's usually a lie. You should say, instead, "It's not important enough for me to *make* the time necessary to do that thing." That may sound extreme, but successful people usually *are* extreme. Successful people are important people whose time is respected by others, because they have done something productive with their lives.

Lessons from Lazarus

> There is time for everything.
> – Thomas Edison

Jesus' friends, Mary and Martha, came to Him one day and told Him that their brother and His friend, Lazarus, was sick, to which Jesus replied, *"It is not a sickness unto death."* Then Lazarus died. Jesus did not attend the funeral or make any contact with the family for several days. When He finally did visit the family in the town of Bethany, Martha rebuked Him for not having intervened to prevent Lazarus' death, to which He replied, *"Your brother will live again."* Martha agreed that Lazarus would live again in the resurrection, but then Jesus replied, *"I am the resurrection!"* Everything Jesus did was holistically educational, and this case was no exception. In this one instance, He demonstrated His authority as the anointed Christ, the triumph of life over death, the power of His words, the fact that He was in constant communication with the Father, His supernatural peace, and His affection, as the Son of Man, for His own friends.

But when He raised His friend who had been dead four days by declaring a sentence that began with the words "I am," He was making a point, among other things, that time was subservient to Him. Jesus said that the sickness was not unto death and, indeed, it *wasn't* unto death, even though Lazarus died! The lesson from the whole thing is that time is irrelevant when it comes to spiritual things. For you, personally, it serves as a reminder that it's never too late for your miracle or breakthrough. You can transcend time by changing the way you think about it and talk about it. You still have time to do great things with your life. You're not too old to see your dreams come true or your vision accomplished. The arrival of the thing for which you have been waiting may seem to you like it's "four days late," but, in actuality, it's probably right on time! Even the things that have begun to decay can live again, as did Lazarus.

The decisions you make today will be the reality in which you walk tomorrow, so you must embrace your time-creativity and seize the day right here and right now! God's original purpose in creation was for His seed to exercise authority and take dominion in the earth (Genesis 1:26-28), and you have been given awesome power to regularly walk in that dominion and to change your world. The good news is that you don't have to wait for time to be on your side to do it. You can take authority over time by living beyond its boundaries altogether. Because you have access to the Keys of the Kingdom, you have a way to unlock the power of *now,* so it's never too late for you to do what you need to do. Destiny is developed one day at a time, and there are more than enough hours in this day to make significant strides toward that end. It's not too late for you to realize your destiny, and it's not too late to realize that *it's all good!*

Meditations for Chapter Seventeen

1.

For a thousand years in Your sight are like yesterday when it is past . . . (Psalms 90:4)

2.

I returned and saw under the sun that – the race is not to the swift, nor the battle to the strong, nor bread to the wise, nor riches to men of understanding, nor favor to men of skill; but TIME AND CHANCE happen to them all. (Ecclesiastes 9:11)

3.

So I will RESTORE TO YOU THE YEARS that the swarming locust has eaten . . . . (Joel 2:25)

4.

See then that you walk circumspectly, not as fools but as wise, REDEEMING THE TIME, because the days are evil. (Ephesians 5:15, 16)

5.

Walk in wisdom toward those who are outside, REDEEMING THE TIME. (Colossians 4:5)

6.

But, beloved, do not forget this one thing, that with the Lord one day is as a thousand years, and a thousand years as one day. (2 Peter 3:8)

7

Blessed is he who reads and those who hear the words of this prophecy, and keep those things which are written in it; for the TIME IS NEAR. (Revelation 1:3)

Chapter Eighteen

Prophetic Realization and Future Realities

And in everything, as we know, He co-operates for good with those who love God and are called according to His purpose.
Romans 8:28 – The New English Bible

> It's never too late to be what you might have been.
> – George Eliot

Prophecy changes things. It opens the passageway between the present and the future. It builds a bridge to destiny and speaks to potential. The order of all things is: the word *first* and *then* the manifestation. In the beginning is always the word. Whether it comes in the form of a word of knowledge or a word of wisdom, prophecy edifies, exhorts and comforts in a way that makes a connection between mouth and heart, mind and spirit, and natural and supernatural. Prophecy confirms what you already know on some level. It may or may not include foretelling or prediction, but a true prophetic utterance will always point you toward the future in some way. Prophecy paints a picture of destiny. It puts a face on the future and brings it closer to perceived reality. Prophecy activates faith and makes it easier to see the invisible. It sets things in motion and is a Kingdom key that unlocks on earth what is unlocked in heaven.

Genesis

CITN was birthed out of a prophecy that confirmed to me a word I received in January, 1985. I spent a great deal of that month in prayer and fasting about the future of my life and ministry, because for the previous five years I had served as my father's associate pastor and I needed to know, for several reasons, if I was where I needed to be or if it was time for a change. It was assumed by everyone at that church (including me) that I would work with him indefinitely and be his successor. In addition to being a full-time pastor (while frequently traveling and ministering elsewhere), I led all of the praise and worship, was the full-time director of a branch of Norvel Hayes Ministries' New Life Bible School, and taught Bible every day in the high school of our A Beka academy. Needless to say, I was very involved with the ministry and the job security it afforded me and my young family was not something that I wanted to lose.

But on the night of January 22, I was praying and said, "Lord, I feel like the people in this church love me, but they don't perceive my gift properly. To them I am the praise and worship leader only, and, even though I 'let no man despise my youth,' I don't believe that I can ever make the transition, in their minds, to become a pastor with a prophetic voice." I don't remember this ever happening to me before or since, but immediately I heard a voice say, *"Turn to Ezekiel 33."* Because Ezekiel is one of my least favorite books, I was quite unfamiliar with its content, but at the end of the chapter were two verses that changed my life: *"Indeed you are to them as a very lovely song of one who has a pleasant voice and can play well on an instrument; for they hear your words, but they do not do them. And when this comes to pass – surely it will come – then they will know that a prophet has been among them" (Ezekiel 33:32, 33).*

To me, this Scripture meant several things, but the main one was that a change was coming. In the back of my mind I had always considered the possibility of starting a church of my own, but I didn't want to hurt my parents in any way by leaving their ministry, so I never moved in that direction. But after that night I began to meditate in the book of Ezekiel and, without telling anyone, started considering the possibility of doing a new thing. For days I read Scriptures in Ezekiel that spoke to me on many levels, but I said nothing about it, not even to those closest to me. Eleven days later, on February 2, I was leading worship for the prophetess Bobbie Jean Merck at a meeting in Augusta, GA. She knew nothing of my Ezekiel Scriptures, but during the meeting she stopped and called me up from the piano I was playing and spoke this prophecy over me:

"There is going to be a new dimension of responsibility that shall be placed upon you as an individual, anointed and called of God, for a unique ministry. And, my son, there shall come upon you a rest in the dimension of the things of the Spirit. And you think that you know what it is to prophesy, **but you shall have now a new anointing that shall be the anointing of Ezekiel.** And as **Ezekiel** was caught up and caught away by the Spirit, and beheld the Son of Man – he beheld the very glory of God – so shall you be caught up, and you shall behold the glory. And you shall see, and you shall converse with the Son of Man.

And an anointing shall arise upon you that you will be able to sit where the people sit, and you will know their going out and their coming in. And it will be said of you, as it was of the prophet of old, 'Surely, the man has been in my bed-chamber, for no one knows that I have done this, or said that.'

But there is a key to this anointing that is coming upon you. And you will have an unction and an anointing from on high to receive from God through an impression, as it were, the key to unlock the doors of men's souls. And you shall be able to go in by the piercing anointing of the Holy Spirit, and you shall speak that key . . . one word sometimes, phrases at other times, and sentences, and yes, even paragraphs at other times . . . to have the anointing that I have said is upon my word, to be sharper than a two-edged sword. It will go in and divide asunder. You'll know, and they'll know.

And as of this hour, this moment in time, though you'll never get away from it . . . **you'll always be my psalmist . . . you'll**

always be my minstrel . . . but, as of David of old, yes, the forehead of David is imparted unto you now. **And they'll no longer know you just as a psalmist, minstrel, or worship leader who prophesies in accuracy. But they'll respect the fivefold offices . . . prophet . . . evangelist . . . pastor . . . teacher. And like the prophet Ezekiel, you'll be used, as he saw it, to cause the free flow of waters to flow from the temple of almighty God. But, yes, says the Spirit of Grace, the highest anointing will be upon prophet.**"

In the mouth of two or three witnesses every word is established, and with this confirmation I began to plan a church that I believed would have prophetic purpose. I went to my father for his blessing, which he gave me, and the rest is history. Not only did the prophecy confirm the Scripture that I had received, but over the years I have seen every part of it fulfilled in some way, especially the part about people saying that I have been in their bed-chamber to hear what they've said. Hardly a week has passed since that time without somebody saying to me, "Have you been bugging my house or my car? What you preached about today was exactly what we were talking about in private!" I hear something to that effect practically all the time. And even though I don't really consider myself to be a prophet, God does seem to use me prophetically in everything that I do in the ministry. *Everything* about CITN is prophetic in nature.

Going Global

On Mother's Day night, May 9, 1999, my friend, and well-known prophet, Dr. Mark Chironna, called me to say, "Jim, I don't know what this means, but I feel impressed to tell you that in the next 11 to 28 days, your church is somehow going to be seen and known all over the world." He didn't have any other details to share with me; he just delivered the message the way the Lord gave it to him and said that he had no idea how it was going to happen. I thanked him for the call, but I certainly couldn't imagine how CITN could gain global exposure in that short amount of time. But I knew that

Mark had been used prophetically in my life before, so I received the word by faith and prepared myself, as much as I could, for what was about to happen in 11 days. I even invited the congregation to come to the church on weekday mornings, for an indefinite period of time, to observe prayer and intercession in preparation for what was on the horizon.

On the morning of May 20, exactly eleven days from Dr. Chironna's phone call (which was one month to the day after the fatal shootings at Columbine High School), a student from Heritage High School in Conyers walked into the school building and opened gunfire on the other students congregating in the commons area. The bullets hit and injured six of them, one of whom was a young woman from our church. The previous day, someone who was attending those morning prayer sessions at the church felt compelled, for some reason, to leave the meeting and drive over to Heritage High just to sit out in front of the building and pray for the protection of the students. I personally believe that it was this person's obedience in prayer that prevented any of the students from being killed that day. Of course, the whole city was immediately in a panic, and the news media from all over the world began to converge upon it.

Before that 11th day was up, because of the young lady who was shot and because of our high profile youth ministry, Teen Planet, our church was seen on all three major networks, *CNN*, and all over the internet. Diane Sawyer, Ted Koppel, and others were calling for interviews and the next morning the church was mentioned on *Good Morning America*. *Fox News* did an entire program from Teen Planet. The following Sunday, all three networks set up satellite links from CITN to broadcast the services, and *Jet Magazine* covered the story. Several days later I met then-Vice President Al Gore, whose first words to me were, "I enjoyed your sermon on Sunday." News people from as far away as Israel called the church for interviews. Later our youth pastor and the young woman who was shot were interviewed in NYC on the *Montel Williams Show*. The prophecy was accurate. Our church had been seen all over the world.

Prior to this happening, I had been trying to get in touch with prophet Kim Clement to invite him to come to the church to minister, and my attempts to connect with him had been unsuccessful. I had sent him a letter, but heard no response. But when he saw on the news what had happened in Conyers, his office called the church to say that he wanted to come as soon as possible, because he had a word for the young people in the area. We agreed on the first available date and, when I counted it up, it was exactly 28 days from Dr. Chironna's phone call. When Kim came to the church, we entered into a season together with his ministry that was unlike anything I had ever experienced before, and it lasted through the turn of the Millennium. In an interview with Matt and Lori Crouch on *TBN*, Kim said they were the greatest meetings he had ever had in his life. It was during that prophetic season that the teaching that became this book was birthed.

Pieces to the Prophetic Puzzle

I don't know how all the pieces of the prophetic puzzle fit into the picture of my life, but I know that prophecy makes things happen and is part of the past-present-future connection. When I was 13 years old, Kathryn Kuhlman kissed me on the cheek and told me that I would minister around the world. When I was 23, Lester Sumrall took me into my dad's office and told me that he wanted to impart to me what Smith Wigglesworth had imparted to him, and he laid hands on me and prayed and prophesied for over an hour. When I was nearly 33, Mike Maiden prophesied that I would be an apostolic father and bishop, when nothing could have been farther from my reality at the time. Some prophecies have been fulfilled, and some are still in the process of fulfillment, but all are significant. A few years ago, Dr. Kelley Varner prophesied that CITN would do something that no church has ever done before, and we are daily in the process of seeing that word come to pass.

Write down all of your prophecies, keep them before your eyes, and pray for discernment in judging them. If a door to the future has opened for you through a prophetic word, walk through it if you can. If you don't understand what it means right now, then the vision may be for an appointed time and you'll have to ponder it in your heart until the season of fulfillment. You can't build your whole life on prophecy, but it certainly can provide important guideposts for you on the road to destiny if you keep it all in perspective. On some level, because *you have what you say*, everything that comes out of your mouth prophetically determines your future in some way. The word is near you, in your mouth and in your heart. The words spoken over your life are part of the things that are working together for your good. The testimony of Jesus is the spirit of prophecy and that testimony is saying to you that *it's all good!*

Meditations for Chapter Eighteen

1.

For I know the thoughts and plans that I have for you, says the Lord, thoughts and plans for welfare and peace and not for evil, to give you hope in your final outcome. (Jeremiah 29:11 AMP)

2.

. . . to another prophetic insight (the gift of interpreting the divine will and purpose) . . . (1 Corinthians 12:10 AMP)

3.

Pursue love, and desire spiritual gifts, but especially that you may prophesy. (1 Corinthians 14:1)

4.

He who speaks in a [strange] tongue edifies and improves himself, but he who prophesies [interpreting the divine will and purpose and teaching with inspiration] edifies and improves the church and promotes growth [in Christian wisdom, piety, holiness, and happiness]. (1 Corinthians 14:4 AMP)

5.

Do not despise prophecies. (1 Thessalonians 5:20)

6.

And so we have the prophetic word confirmed, which you do well to heed as a light that shines in a dark place, until the day dawns and the morning star rises in your hearts. (2 Peter 1:19)

7.

And I fell at his feet to worship him. But he said to me, "See that you do not do that! I am your fellow servant, and of your brethren who have the testimony of Jesus. Worship God! For the testimony of Jesus is the spirit of prophecy." (Revelation 19:10)

Chapter Nineteen

Reversing the Order of the Universe

Yes, we know that all things go on working together for the good of those who keep on loving God, who are called in accordance with God's purpose.
Romans 8:28 – The New Testament:
A Translation in the Language of the People
(Charles B. Williams)

> Doctors and scientists said that breaking the four-minute mile was impossible, that one would die in the attempt. Thus, when I got up from the track after collapsing at the finish line, I figured I was dead.
> – Roger Bannister (after becoming the first person to break the four-minute mile in 1952)

All things are possible for those who believe. Regardless of the perceived limitations that you have either collected or discovered during your lifetime, you were *meant* to spend your time here in the pursuit of living a life with no limitations – one that establishes and confirms on a regular basis that, through experience, miracles really do happen every day. It is your responsibility to determine what it is you want to do and then ***do it,*** defying the odds and proving that, if God is for you, no one can actually be against you. The decision not to fail is entirely yours. In faith, you have a mandate to direct your life forward, to diligently pursue your goals and to prove to yourself, and those around you, that you *can do* all things through Christ Who strengthens you. Your life must become both the prayer for the impossible and the sermon that exemplifies and illustrates that prayer. It must be transformed into the word made flesh.

Just because someone *says* that something can't be done doesn't *mean* that it can't be done. We live in a world where records are broken every day, where long-held beliefs are regularly disproved, and where new information constantly replaces long-accepted ways of doing things. You must constantly rethink the world to be able to keep up with it, and being led by the Spirit enables you to know when to deliberately change things as they currently are and when to just go with the flow. Miracles are simply the suspension of natural law, and natural law was *created* to be suspended. In the same way that Moses' law was instituted to force us into grace, the laws of nature were made to force us into the miraculous. Old Testament law revealed the necessity of a Christ who could fulfill it, and natural law operates for the very same purpose. Jesus reversed the old order and religious system, and He is still doing it through His Christ in the 21st century.

The Backwards Kingdom

I was born backwards. Because of the shape and size of my mother's womb, I was unable to turn and get into a proper birth position, as a fetus is supposed to do prior to labor. So, instead of coming through the birth canal head first, I came out feet first. Actually, I came out *foot* first, which greatly compromised my chances for survival, because during the time it took for the doctor to make contact with my other "unborn" foot, I practically drowned in the amniotic fluid. Because I was born without caesarian section, my unusual breach birth was witnessed by an entire class of medical students. I was literally born in front of an audience, which may account for my never once having had stage fright in my life. *And* I was born in the wrong direction, which may account for the fact that I usually see things differently than most people see them, and do and say things that cause me to always swim upstream and go against the grain.

I was unable to make any sound whatsoever for the first several days of my life (which may also account for why I've had so much to say since then) and later suffered many respiratory complications from the weakened condition of my fluid-filled lungs. On one hand, I'm being facetious when I say that being born differently or backwards was significant for my life. On the other hand, when I consider Biblical examples of significant births (like Jacob coming out of the womb holding Esau's heal), I think that maybe it had symbolic meaning, after all. Whatever the case, the whole experience was quite traumatic, physically and emotionally, for my then 19-year-old mother, and is the reason I'm an only child. And *any* only child will tell you that they always felt very different from other kids, and usually found it difficult to assimilate. Add to that the fact that I am left-handed and extremely right-brained, and you have a recipe for a backwards life.

I believe that this is why the "different-ness" of the Kingdom gospel makes so much sense to me and why my theology, though technically orthodox, is rarely, if ever, mainstream. Dony and Reba (Rambo) McGuire wrote an excellent song several years ago called *Backwards Kingdom*, which explores with great insight, the illogical, "backward" nature of the Kingdom of God.* It's a beautiful national anthem for spiritual Israel. Such themes as "the first shall be last, and the last shall be first" are the building blocks of the Kingdom. In God, the way up is down. In Christ, the way to rule is to serve. In the Spirit, the way to live is to die. Logic says *a penny saved is a penny earned*, but God says *give, and it shall be given to you*. It's all backwards, which is why you have to repent (which simply means to reverse your direction) to enter into it. This kind of repentance is more than just thinking outside the box.

*Many of Dony and Reba's songs have been inspired by the ministry of my uncle, Bishop Earl Paulk, and the Cathedral of the Holy Spirit. The very talented Anthony Lockett from the Cathedral also wrote a song, similarly inspired, entitled *Upside Down Kingdom*.

Never Say Never

Repentance isn't easy. It requires much less effort to just flow with the current of the world's system. But the reason it is so important to embrace the "backward-ness" of the Kingdom is that it sets the course for the miraculous. You can turn things around in your life and reverse the order of past generations by seeking first the Kingdom. In a sense, the suspension of natural law is reversing the order of the universe. When Jesus walked on water, He reversed the order of the law of gravity. When He healed the sick and raised the dead, He reversed the order of disease and all works of the curse. The Kingdom suffers violence and the violent take it by force, so don't be passive and never confuse contentment with complacency. You must take the miraculous by force. Going with the flow is important, but sometimes you are responsible for *releasing* the flow! Believe in God and believe in yourself. Believe in what can happen right now!

Never say that something is impossible. You live in a world where anything can happen at any time and every wrong thing in your life is a set up for a miracle! Stay prepared in your attitude, and *especially* by the words of your mouth, for the imminent miraculous. Your whole world can change in a day. To them that have, more will be given, so keep attracting the supernatural to yourself by thinking differently and staying open to the supernatural. When Jesus spoke, people said that no one ever spoke like Him. And because He spoke differently, He could do the unordinary and the unprecedented. You were not made to be common. Your faith makes you special, so use it to its greatest advantage and do what hasn't been done before. Dare to be different. Dare to believe. Dare to challenge natural laws. Anything can happen, but whatever *does* happen will work together for your good. Miraculously, **it's *all* good!**

Meditations for Chapter Nineteen

1.

Of old You laid the foundation of the earth, and the heavens are the work of Your hands. They will perish, but You will endure; Yes, they will grow old like a garment; like a cloak You will change them, and they will be changed. (Psalm 102:25, 26)

2

Ah, Lord God! Behold, You have made the heavens and the earth by Your great power and outstretched arm. There is nothing too hard for You. (Jeremiah 32:17)

3.

*But Jesus looked at them and said to them, "With men this is impossible, but with God all things are possible."
(Matthew 19:26)*

4.

*But Jesus looked at them and said, "With men it is impossible, but not with God; for with God all things are possible."
(Mark 10:27)*

5.

For with God nothing will be impossible. (Luke 1:37)

6

But He said, "The things which are impossible with men are possible with God." (Luke 18:27)

7.

But when they did not find them, they dragged Jason and some brethren to the rulers of the city, crying out, "These who have turned the world upside down have come here too." (Acts 17:6)

Chapter Twenty

Coming Full Circle

We know also that those who love God, those who have been called in terms of His purpose, have His aid and interest in everything.

Romans 8:28 – Moffatt

> He who would learn to fly one day must first learn to stand and walk and run and climb and dance; one cannot fly into flying.
>
> – Friedrich Nietzsche

I rarely refer to the 1611 edition of the King James Version (what the mainstream calls the "Authorized Version"), because, as any true linguist knows, it is nowhere near being the best translation, and the wording is basically irrelevant to modern-thinking people. But there is one Elizabethan word that I really like a lot, which made its way into the better translated New King James Version: the word *circumspect.* It's found in two places: *"And in all that I have said to you, be circumspect and make no mention of the name of the other gods, nor let it be heard from your mouth" (Exodus 23:13)*, and *"See then that you walk circumspectly, not as fools but as wise" (Ephesians 5:15)*. Derived from the Latin *circumspectus*, it is defined as "to take heed of circumstances or future consequences." Modern Bible translations say to "walk carefully," but I like *circumspect*, because it literally means "to see in a circle."

To me, the concept of circular vision is having the ability to look at the past, present and future from one vantage point, which is the *now.* Being circumspect means being carefully aware, but you can only be that way by seeing and learning from your *whole* life experience. Seeing in a circle is perceiving eternity, recognizing the cyclical nature of events that simply seem serendipitous on the surface, but are actually part of a bigger plan. Co-centric circles of occurrences continually work together for your good, growing larger and larger as you ascend from glory to glory. As your capacity for revelation increases, the small circles gradually evolve so that, little by little, you are able to move into your destiny's broader context. You have to walk before you can run, and what may seem to you as your being stuck moving round and round the same cycle, may actually be the way for you to spiral upwards into all that God has for you.

Will the Circle Be Unbroken?

Before either Debye or I were born, we had a cosmic connection on the circle of life. Back in the early '50's, my dad, who was a college student at the time, was driving back to his school in Tennessee through the mountains of north Georgia. He had gone to Tampa, FL to visit my mom for the weekend and, after having been on the road for many long hours, got caught in a terrible rainstorm in the middle of the night on a dark and remote section of mountain highway. Rounding a curve too fast, he lost control of the car, veered off the road and plummeted, end over end for hundreds of feet, down to the bottom of a heavily wooded ravine in the middle of nowhere. On impact, he was partially thrown from the car, which landed on his leg and pinned it in the closed door of the driver's side. He was trapped in the car at the bottom of the mountain. He lay there for hours in the inky blackness of the rainy night, slowly bleeding to death.

The part of the woods where his car landed was so out of the way that other cars had eventually been found in the same area containing the skeletons of drivers who had previously driven off the same mountain. Because he couldn't pry himself out of the car door, and because he was sure that he would die before he was ever found, my dad found a piece of paper in the car, scribbled a good-bye note to be found by whomever might finally happen upon him, and slipped into unconsciousness. But, amazingly, at the break of dawn he was discovered and rescued by a pair of hunters who just happened to be trekking through the extremely remote area. He was hospitalized and then walked on crutches for awhile before receiving a dramatic healing in his broken leg one day on his college campus. The whole thing was incredible, and I have heard him tell the story of his miraculous rescue and healing many times throughout my life.

Some years after Debye and I were married, we were spending time with my parents one day and, in conversation, she was telling us about her best friend in high school whose family owned a home in a town in the north Georgia mountains. She told us about how she and her friend used to drive up to the mountains on weekends and stay at the family's vacation home. When she happened to mention her friend's very uncommon last name, my dad recognized it as the last name of the man who had saved his life over fifty years earlier. The place where his wreck had taken place was right outside the little town where Debye's friend's family had lived and, when we put all the facts together, we discovered that Debye's friend's grandfather had apparently saved my dad's life, years before either she or I were born! It was an important addition to an already amazing story, confirming the fact that the circle of life is a very small world!

A few years after that, a long-time friend and neighbor of Debye's parents passed away and, in conversation with the man's widow, my mother-in-law discovered that my great-grandfather on my mother's side (who died before I was born) had performed their wedding ceremony in south Georgia in the late 40's! Debye's family had lived across the street from them for years and had never discovered that connection. So she and I were linked through both my dad *and* my mom long before we ever met. I also have many similar stories of colliding histories and interconnected destinies with several people in our church. The whole concept of "six degrees of separation," or that everyone on earth is only separated by a maximum of six relationships, is not just interesting, it's actually plausible! Coming full circle in your life can mean many things, but one definite meaning is that the relationships and events of your life are all positioned around one giant ring.

I'll See You Later

In my very early teen years, the walls of my room were covered with posters and memorabilia and in the middle of it all hung a cover from the October 25, 1971 issue of *Time* magazine. It showed a picture of a young man named Jeff Fenholt in costume as Jesus, and the headline across his image read *"Jesus Christ Superstar Rocks Broadway."* Jeff was starring as Jesus in the controversial, smash-hit rock opera at the Mark Hellinger Theatre, a role made famous by the enormously successful studio concert album released a couple of years earlier. Ian Gillan, the lead singer from Deep Purple, had sung the part of Jesus on the initial album, but Jeff played the character on Broadway. I had (and loved) both the concert album and the original Broadway cast album (with Jeff). I really liked Jeff's picture on the cover of the magazine, and it hung on my wall until I went away to college.

Years later I heard that the young man from that magazine cover had become a Christian and was in the ministry. He had had a brief connection with the 80's incarnation of Black Sabbath, but I remembered him from *Superstar* and was excited about what I heard had happened to him. One day I learned that he was going to be appearing with Pat Robertson on *The 700 Club*, so I tuned in to see him. I greatly enjoyed his interview, but imagine my *complete shock* when he stood up to sing a song that *I* had written! As the music from his track began to play, I immediately recognized the arrangement as that of Candi Staton's version of a song I had written in 1980 called *"It's the Anointing."* I couldn't believe what I was hearing and had no idea how he would have found my song. The Broadway star whose picture I had looked at for years, and whose album I had played thousands of times, was singing *my song!*

To make a very long story short, I eventually met Jeff at a tribute to Dottie Rambo in Nashville, told him that I had written *The Anointing*, invited him to come to CITN, which He did, and we eventually became good friends. The first time he came to minister, he told me to keep the offering that came in for him that night, in symbolic payment and appreciation for all the tapes and CDs he had sold with my song, because he hadn't known until he met me that I had written it. He also told me that, of all the songs he had ever recorded, secular or spiritual, *It's the Anointing* was his favorite. In time, I found out that my favorite artist, Salvador Dali, had been one of Jeff's closest friends and that he had lived in Dali's castle in Spain. The whole thing was very cool, of course, but, on a deeper level, it made me aware of how many other things like that had happened in my life – things that show how significant events move in a circle.

Nearly 30 years after I bought the *Superstar* cast album, I finally got the star to autograph it for me. Some things are introduced into our lives for a reason, but we don't understand why until much later – until the arc is completed and our lives come around in a complete orbit. What goes around comes around and, in the spirit realm, time is much more cyclical than it is linear. I don't know how to better explain this, so you'll just have to hear and comprehend it by the Spirit, but all things work together for good *in a circle*. The earth is round and it revolves and rotates on its axis, which is why we have the continuing cycle of days and seasons. The sowing and reaping principle works in a never-ending circle of life. Eternity (or *now*) is in a circle, because it has no beginning and no ending. There are things in your life right now that will not have great meaning for you until much later – until after you have completed a full revolution.

The Renewal of Your Youth

Youth is not entirely a time of life; it is a state of mind. Nobody grows old by merely living a number of years. People grow old by deserting their ideals. You are as young as your faith, as old as your doubt; as young as your self-confidence, as old as your fear; as young as your hope, as old as your despair.

– Douglas MacArthur

One last and very important aspect of coming full circle is having your youth renewed. Jesus said you must become like a child to enter the Kingdom. He went even further than that when He told Nicodemus that he should be "born again." Usually we hear the concept of the revisiting of youth mentioned in a negative light. When someone is acting immaturely they are called *childish*, and it's not meant to be complimentary. When an elderly person manifests senility, they are often said to be in their second childhood, and it's not a positive thing. But all the hopes and ideals and innocence of your youth are still resident in your eternal life and can be spiritually unlocked to affect you favorably. The good part of the past is still in you. Tap into it. Revisit the person that you were *before* you were cynical or bitter or emotionally damaged, and let that person influence who you are now. Your life is coming full circle, and **it's all good!**

Meditations for Chapter Twenty

1.
Who satisfies your mouth with good things,
so that your youth is renewed like the eagle's.
(Psalms 103:5)

2.

*Even the youths shall faint and be weary, and the young
men shall utterly fall, but those who wait on the Lord
shall renew their strength; They shall mount up with
wings like eagles, they shall run and not be weary, they
shall walk and not faint.*
(Isaiah 40:30, 31)

3.

*. . . the disciples came to Jesus asking, "Who gets the
highest rank in God's kingdom?" For an answer Jesus
called over a child, whom He stood in the middle of
the room, and said, "I'm telling you, once and for all,
that unless you return to square one and start over
like children, you're not even going to get a look at the
kingdom, let alone get in. Whoever becomes simple and
elemental again, like this child, will rank high in God's
kingdom. What's more, when you receive the childlike
on my account, it's the same as receiving me."*
(Matthew 18:1-5 The Message)

4.

*One day children were brought to Jesus in the hope that
He would lay hands on them and pray over them. The
disciples shooed them off. But Jesus intervened: "Let
the children alone, don't prevent them from coming to
me. God's kingdom is made up of people like these."*
(Matthew 19:13, 14 The Message)

5.

*Watch what God does, and then do it, like children who
learn proper behavior from their parents.*
(Ephesians 5:1 The Message)

6.

*See then that you walk circumspectly, not as fools but
as wise, redeeming the time, because the days are evil.*
(Ephesians 5:15, 16)

7.

*As obedient children, let yourselves be pulled into a way
of life shaped by God's life, a life energetic and blazing
with holiness. (1 Peter 1:15 The Message)*

Chapter Twenty-One

The Future is Now!

And we know that all things work together for good to those who love God, to those who are the called according to His purpose.

Romans 8:28 – NKJV

> The present was an egg laid by the past that had the future in it.
>
> – Zora Neale Hurston

And so we have come to the end of the book but not to the end of the journey. We've discussed many things, but it all comes back to the concept of *now*. Now is what matters. The seeds of the future are in your *now* and that's why we've covered time-traveling and truth-telling, the healing of old wounds, and forgiveness. We've discussed imagination and faith and possibilities and prophetic realization, and the bottom line is: the future is now! I've ended each of the previous twenty chapters with seven verses of Scripture on which to meditate, and I hope you didn't overlook them. They are there for a reason, and you may need to go back and consider them, especially if you didn't pay attention to them before. I've ended this chapter, however, with seven affirmations that I trust will be helpful to you. There is nothing as powerful as the spoken word. It's what God used to create everything and how He holds it all together.

Tying Up Loose Ends

In Chapter Two, I discussed how I felt about being named for my father and my uncle, but I would be remiss not to take this opportunity to say how I really feel about both of them, as well as the other people who have significantly influenced my life. Each of us is a composite of all the people that we have known. We are all connected, and understanding that connection is a vital part of knowing how all things work together for our good. I have wonderful friends and an amazing staff and board of directors and ministry of helps. I am blessed to be able to provide covering for great pastors and ministers whom I love and respect. With my congregation and extended family, I am surrounded by beautiful people who love me and bless my life, and I don't take any of them for granted. Even my enemies have helped me to become who I am, so I gladly feast at the table that God has spread for me in their presence.

My father was a very strict disciplinarian, as was his father, and in his younger days was a strong, imposing, often intimidating presence to me. But as time has passed, he has moved toward me by mellowing with age; I have moved toward him by growing to appreciate his powerful personality; and we have met somewhere in the middle. He is a much better preacher than I will ever be and has a speaking voice that will always be superior to mine. He has had more success than he gives himself credit for having, throughout a ministry that has been consistently fruitful for more than half a century. He has built churches, excelled in radio and on television, enjoyed a long career as an executive official in his denomination, was the first Pentecostal president of the Atlanta Christian Council, and has preached in churches on every continent of the earth, including the world's largest in Seoul, Korea. He has been faithfully married to my mother for the majority of both their lives.

My mother is more than a woman; she is a veritable force of femininity. Married at age 17 to the only man she ever dated, she has always supported his ministry without reservation, and they are more in love with each other now than they ever were. Ordained as a minister under my covering, she is passionate about the things she believes. And although we do not always see eye to eye, theologically, I respect the fact that she is not easily moved, doctrinally, not even by me. She is a very good pastor – in some ways, better than I. She is artistic and creative and has a razor sharp sense of humor that can still crack me up. Hopefully, I have picked up the positive aspects of both my parents and have made them proud of me. They have never been anything but helpful and supportive, and unselfishly giving to Debye, to our kids, and to CITN. When I look at our relationship at this point, I can say "it's all good."

My Uncle Earl will definitely not like what I said about him earlier, but the truth is that I am awed by him in many ways. People are always talking about him, but whatever has been said that is or isn't true about his personal life is between him and God. The fact is that he has influenced the modern church more than can be appreciated at this point, and he has made the gospel of the Kingdom a reality because of his courage to preach it. I am always amazed at how he has been able to reinvent himself and survive things that would devastate the average person. But I am most appreciative of the way that he has confronted racism (which I believe is one of the worst sins tolerated by the church) and how he has been able to remain ahead of his time, theologically. At this point, we are not really close, and what I said earlier about our connection closing doors for me was not said out of bitterness – it is simply the truth. But I will always respect what he has accomplished.

Bringing It Home

My in-laws, Bo and Shirley Flanders, are honest, good-hearted, hard-working, unpretentious, "salt of the earth" kind of people. I have to mention them before I say something about Debye, because if they had not adopted her at birth, I might not be where I am today. Back then, they thought they were just getting a baby (they have always adored her, and still do), but they were actually helping to fulfill Kingdom purposes without knowing it. I say that because, if they hadn't found her, I might not have ever met and married her, and I might not be in the ministry today. Both of them have worked for and supported my ministry since Debye and I were married, and my mother-in-law might just be my biggest fan. They are true, selfless givers in every sense of the word. Both they and my parents have always been excellent grandparents, and my kids are blessed to have them in their lives and to have a relationship with each of them.

My soul mate, Debye, is beautiful and smart and cool and anointed. A wonderful wife, incredible mother, effective pastor, first-rate administrator . . . she is simply a great woman. She is a voracious reader, has incredible instincts, and possesses a sense of style that sets her apart from the ordinary. I have seen her navigate a Greek oil tanker through the locks of the Panama Canal (I'm not kidding), play hostess to 2,500 people who came through our home in one evening (seriously), and literally perform miracles with finances, both for us personally and for the church. She seems to become more gorgeous with age and generally makes the virtuous woman of Proverbs 31 look lazy. She practices what she preaches, has great strength of character, walks in the Spirit, (drives too fast), and is a role model, not just for women, but for people in general. She has influenced me, taught me, inspired me, and is a part of me in every way.

I already wrote about my four kids in my first book, *Activating the Power of Life and Death,* and I could go on about others who have helped make me what I am, but I've got to end this book! I will, however, mention one other person who has influenced me in recent years and that is my friend, Ryan Klesko. I first met him when he played ball for the Atlanta Braves, before being traded to the San Diego Padres. Ryan is not only a professional athlete who has had a great career, but he is truly a man's man who lives to hunt, fish, surf and such things as that. I would have never thought that we would be friends, because I don't do *any* of those things. However, he patiently taught me how to shoot a gun and how to hunt (I killed a wild boar that weighed nearly 300 pounds on my first trip), and, even though it hasn't really awakened my "inner hunter," it did trigger something in me that I had never experienced prior to knowing him. His friendship, and all that comes with it, has helped me to explore a part of being a man that I had never tapped into before. It has allowed me to become comfortable just being one of the guys.

But, What About Me?

> Life can be found only in the present moment. The past is gone, the future is not yet here, and if we do not go back to ourselves in the present moment, we cannot be in touch with life.
>
> – Thich Nhat Hanh

You may ask at this point what all this has to do with a chapter entitled *The Future is Now,* and, more importantly, what it has to do with you. The point is that the seeds of the future lie in the present, and your perception of the present is made up of what you have learned from the past, and what you have learned has come, most likely, through your relationships. So, embrace the ones you have *now.* Appreciate them *now.* Love them *now.* Tell them how you feel about them *now.* They may be here to help you to determine the quality of your future, and time travel is more enjoyable when you have traveling partners. New Age guru, Wayne Dyer, says "Go for it now. The future is promised to no one." And even though I do believe that you have a future, it is a good idea to live like you don't. By that I mean, if you put some things off 'til tomorrow, you may not have the chance to get them done. Believing that the future is now means living fully today.

My first words to you in the introduction to this book were in the form of the question: Do you know who you are? I hope that these pages have helped you to better understand how to answer that question for yourself and that you will want to refer to them again and again in the future. But no book or teaching or sermon can fully answer that question for you. On some level, you will be searching for the complete answer throughout the entire journey of your life. If you choose to see the quest for holistic identity as a great adventure, you will enjoy the whole process a lot more. And the better you understand yourself, the better you will be able to understand God and His plan for your life. Remember that wisdom has built her house on seven pillars and there is always room for you in the house that wisdom builds. Those seven pillars provide a strong foundation for a life that, in the final analysis, really is all good.

Personally, even *with* the accessibility of the wisdom of God, most of the time I feel like the more I know, the less I know. There are so many things to consider about life, and how the past, present and future work together, that it's easy to feel conflicted about knowing the right way to look at it all. Predestination, foreknowledge, the sovereignty of God, election, the perfect will of God, God's ultimate purpose – these themes and concepts are baffling and interesting and confusing and wonderful, all at the same time. In the real world there are some days when it seems to you that there really is no big picture and that most of the things that happen in your life are just random and disconnected and generally meaningless. But then something amazing will occur that you know is beyond coincidence, fluke, or happenstance, and you see the hand of God supernaturally intervene in a situation, and suddenly you look at everything differently.

The eighth chapter of Romans is my favorite in the Bible. I encourage you to study it in its entire context to better understand verse 28 and how all things work together for your good. Much of what you can't explain or articulate about your real needs and desires is the product of those "groanings that cannot be uttered" mentioned in verse 26, which are really the Holy Spirit's intercession for your life. I've tried to *utter* as much as I can here to help you, but the Spirit will have to help you with the rest, and He will if you just ask Him. He's always standing by to help you figure it all out. He will help you move from *thinking* you are to *knowing* you are. So don't ever give up on your search for answers. As long as you still have questions that need to be answered, you still have a reason to keep living. Embrace your whole life, always looking for what is good in the past, present, and future of it. Don't grow weary in your search, because there's a lot to be learned, and *it's all* . . . well, you know.

Meditations for Chapter Twenty One:

AFFIRMATIONS

Affirmation I   –   The Past

Affirmation II   –   The Present

Affirmation III   –   The Future

Affirmation IV   –   Now

Affirmation V   –   This

Affirmation VI   –   My Life

Affirmation VII   –   Today

Affirmation I: The Past

The past is my teacher.
The past is not my master.
The past does not determine my future.
The past is behind me.
The past has made me strong.
The past cannot hold me back.
The past does not own me.

I can let yesterday go.
I am moving on.
I will not live in regret.
I forgive everyone.
I release all bitterness.
I release all disappointment.
I have learned my lessons well.

No painful memory can stop me.
No guilt from the past can oppress me.
No memory of failure can shake my confidence.
No old, negative thoughts can imprison me.
No chains of shame can bind me.
No regrets can limit me.
No turning back for me.

Affirmation II: The Present

The present has great potential for my life.
The present has unlimited possibilities for me.
The present has promise for the future.
The present is revealing purpose in me.
The present is the point of my focus.
The present offers me a clean slate.
The present is blessed with God's presence.

I have a good feeling about my current circumstances.
I have a positive outlook on things as they are.
I am content with what I have.
I am patient in tribulation.
I am at peace with myself.
I am grateful.
I trust in God.

It's a great time to be alive.
It's my finest hour.
It's my intention to stay in the moment.
It's my plan to "stop and smell the roses."
It's possible with God.
It's my turn.
It's all good!

Affirmation III: The Future

The future will explain my past.
The future will confirm my present.
The future looks good to me.
The future will reveal the answers to my prayers.
The future will fulfill my personal prophecies.
The future is covered in intercession.
The future is full of promise.

I am not afraid of the future.
I do not dread what's ahead of me.
I am not worried about tomorrow.
I am getting better with age.
I am moving forward.
I am going from glory to glory.
I have everything to look forward to.

My latter will be greater than my former.
My goals are attainable.
My dreams can come true.
My vision will be realized.
My future is in God's hands.
My future is very, very bright.
My best days are ahead of me.

Affirmation IV: Now

Now is the time for blessings.
Now is where the I AM is revealed.
Now is eternal.
Now is where I live.
Now is what I believe in.
Now is full of possibility.
Now faith is.

I will embrace the now.
I will not be bound to the past by regret.
I will not be preoccupied by worry about the future.
I will update my thinking.
I will keep an open mind.
I will not resist change.
I am flexible.

The place of manifestation is in the now.
The peace that passes understanding is in the now.
The path of life is in the now.
The harmony of the universe is in the now.
The center of my joy is in the now.
The Kingdom is coming in the now.
The Christ is revealed in the now.

Affirmation V: This

This is the day the Lord has made.
This is the best time of my life.
This is the greatest time to be alive.
This is what I am excited about.
This is what I've been waiting for.
This is where destiny is revealed.
This is it!

*The miracle is **this.***
The time is now.
The place is here.
The provision is already mine.
The way has already been made.
The Kingdom of God is at hand.
The best is yet to come.

I will play well the hand that has been dealt me.
I will work with what I have.
I will not complain about what I don't have.
I will maximize the moment.
I will discern my window of opportunity.
I will recognize the power of what I have in my hand.
*I will not miss **this** by looking for **that.***

Affirmation VI: My Life

My life has purpose.
My life has meaning.
My life counts.
My life matters.
My life is important to God.
My life is important to others.
My life is unique.

I was born by divine design.
I am here for a reason.
I will realize my destiny.
I will live the life I was meant to live.
I will walk in my calling.
I will love and cherish my life.
I will never envy anyone else's life.

The will of God is being done in my life.
The course of my life is moving in the right direction.
The plan for my life is unfolding.
The best part of my life is still ahead of me.
The path before me is clear.
The story of my life will have a happy ending.
The world is a better place because I am here.

Affirmation: VII: Today

Today I will recognize my opportunities.
Today I will have a good attitude.
Today I will be optimistic.
Today I will succeed.
Today I will be in the flow.
Today is filled with possibilities.
Today is my day.

I will make the most of my time today.
I will not waste my time on unimportant things.
I will recognize the beauty around me today.
I will be thankful today.
I will think positively today.
I will be a blessing to someone today.
I will seize this day, completely.

God is helping me today.
God is my rock today.
God is on my side today.
God is blessing me today.
God is protecting me today.
God is defending me today.
God is working all things together for my good today!

Other Books by Bishop Swilley . . .

Keepin' It Real

**Becoming a Real Person,
Experiencing the Real God,
in the Real World**

You've never read a book quite like *Keepin' It Real!* In its pages, Bishop Swilley candidly examines an unusually wide array of subjects . . . the reality TV phenomenon . . . pop culture . . . history . . . politics . . . self-esteem . . . prosperity . . . success . . . parenting . . . multiculturalism . . . New Age philosophy . . . world religions . . . political correctness . . . racism . . . sexism . . . tolerance . . . activism . . . technology . . . addiction . . . eschatology . . . dispensationalism . . . the antichrist . . . orthodoxy . . . prayer . . . the Holy Spirit . . . destiny . . . purpose . . . vision . . . and much more . . . and addresses how they all relate to the Kingdom of God in the now!

But *Keepin' it Real* is also about *you* and how you can develop the courage and confidence to be yourself at all times and to live your *real* life without compromise. Socially relevant, thought-provoking, and theologically edgy, *Keepin' it Real* is a modern manifesto for REAL PEOPLE EXPERIENCING THE REAL GOD IN THE REAL WORLD.

If you're ready to get *real*, get this book!

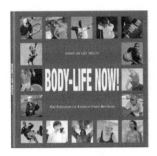

Body-Life Now!
Mini-Meditations for Maximum Fitness Motivation

Whether you're a serious body builder, competitive athlete, or just somebody who wants to drop a few pounds and be a little healthier than you are now, this power-devotional is for you! Inside you'll find 75 crisp little meditations on fitness, nutrition, attitude and lifestyle that will supercharge your workout and improve your outlook on your day.

You'll be doing yourself a big favor by incorporating these inspiring pages into your regular routine, *however* you choose to do so. Your spirit will be refreshed, your mind will be sharpened, and your body will thank you for the extra empowerment.

And if you're just getting *started* on the road to physical fitness, you'll find this book to be *especially* beneficial. It will serve as an easy-to-read road map for the journey designed to help you discover the new, improved *you.*

That journey can start right here . . . and it can start right *NOW!*

Activating the Power of Life and Death

It's Your Life . . .
It's Your Choice . . .
YOU CHOOSE!

God has given you the power to choose life or death, blessing or cursing. By the words of your mouth, you determine the quality of your life. This powerful book will help put you in charge of your life and future.

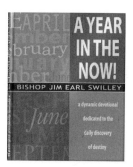

A Year In The Now!

a dynamic devotional dedicated to the daily discovery of destiny.

Would you like to . . .

. . . discover your destiny?
. . . perceive your purpose?
. . . validate your vision?
. . . reinforce your relationships?
. . . strengthen your self-esteem?
. . . overcome your obstacles?
. . . feed your faith?

You can . . . this year!
You can . . . by living in the now!
You can . . . one day at a time!

God is on your side! He is available to assist you in the pursuit of your potential as you develop the diligence to seriously search out your personal path for growth into greatness! Through seeking first His Kingdom and righteousness, you can become the person that He created you to be!

You can ONLY find God's Kingdom in the eternal "NOW" as you endeavor to experience Him in your everyday existence. Kingdom-seeking consists of a constant effort to embrace the now and a commitment to the continual conforming of your consciousness to it. This empowers and enables you to escape the mental distractions produced by living in the past or in the future, so that you can comprehend a real Christ for your current real circumstances!

A YEAR IN THE NOW! is a devotional designed to deliver a doable format for the daily development of your eternal life – to help you think creatively, beyond your familiar, time-bound comfort zones. These positive and powerful affirmations will provide the help you need to progressively put your life on the right track in realistic increments. You don't have to become overwhelmed by the tremendous task of trying to lead a "now life" in a "yesterday/ tomorrow world." You can do it day by day!

This is your year to change your world! You can change your world by changing your mind! You can change your mind one day at a time!

It's time for a fresh start, and you can start right NOW!

What others have to say about *A Year In The Now!* . . .

When my dear friend, Bishop Jim Swilley sent me a copy of his new daily devotional, *A Year In The Now!*, I stopped everything I was doing and couldn't put it down . . . that is until my wife took it out of my hands and I have had to pry it back from her ever since. Jim is one of the most effective, prolific, and unique communicators I have ever met. He breaks down deep and profound truth and makes it palatable for all of us in such a practical way that just reading the principles and reciting the affirmations increases our life skills. The days are broken down into seven key principles a day, seven being the number of alignment between heaven and earth (4 being the number of earth, and three of heaven), whereby applying the seven daily truths your heart and mind are aligned with heaven's best and you are automatically brought into the kind of agreement that gets results in your life. If you want to get the "more" out of your daily life that has been promised to you in Christ I want to encourage you to get your hands on *A Year In The Now! and make it a part of your daily spiritual discipline and focus. Oh yea, and if anyone else gets their hands on your copy in your family . . . buy another one because you won't get it back quick enough!*

Dr. Mark J. Chironna
The Master's Touch International Church
Orlando, Florida

Your devotional, *A Year in the Now!,* reads as a personal message to me. Each day I am encouraged - God is doing a new thing in the NOW! This devotional reinforces that God is working His plan in all things that affect my family and ministry. My destiny continues to unfold so that others will see my good works and glorify the Father.

Germaine Copeland
Author of Prayers That Avail Much Family Books

Deeply profound, yet 'DO-ably' practical. That's how I describe Bishop Jim Earl Swilley's *A Year In The Now! daily devotional. Bishop Jim's 'easy to read' style of communication, combined with his witty grouping together of words that start with the same letter, define this devotional as a delightful way to delve deeper into your divine destiny as a daily discipline. Profound and practical, it's the perfect proponent to promote your personal progress.*

Doug Fortune
Trumpet Call Ministry

A Year In The Now! by Bishop Jim Earl Swilley, is extraordinary and powerful, giving day by day guidance on how to be strong in the Lord through seven pearls of wisdom each day. Seven! This is God's number for completeness and fulfillment. Through A Year In The Now!, God is truly using Bishop Swilley in a mighty way to unlock the wonderful mystery of the gospel so that each of us can live abundantly, and serve God abundantly, in the now!

David Scott
United States Congressman, Georgia

To receive a full listing of Bishop
Swilley's products, write or call:

CITN Media Group
P.O. Box 80876
Conyers, GA 30013

Phone: 678-607-3113
Fax: 770-922-5337
E-mail: products@churchinthenow.org

or visit our website:
www.churchinthenow.org